Augmented Reality

T0045388

Augmented Reality

Unboxing Tech's Next Big Thing

Mark Pesce

polity

Copyright © Mark Pesce 2021

The right of Mark Pesce to be identified as Author of this Work has been asserted in accordance with the UK Copyright, Designs and Patents Act 1988.

First published in 2021 by Polity Press

Polity Press
65 Bridge Street
Cambridge CB2 1UR, UK

Polity Press
101 Station Landing
Suite 300
Medford, MA 02155, USA

All rights reserved. Except for the quotation of short passages for the purpose of criticism and review, no part of this publication may be reproduced, stored in a retrieval system or transmitted, in any form or by any means, electronic, mechanical, photocopying, recording or otherwise, without the prior permission of the publisher.

ISBN-13: 978-1-5095-4093-8
ISBN-13: 978-1-5095-4094-5 (pb)

A catalogue record for this book is available from the British Library.

Typeset in 11 on 14pt Sabon
by Fakenham Prepress Solutions, Fakenham, Norfolk NR21 8NL
Printed and bound in Great Britain by TJ International Limited

The publisher has used its best endeavours to ensure that the URLs for external websites referred to in this book are correct and active at the time of going to press. However, the publisher has no responsibility for the websites and can make no guarantee that a site will remain live or that the content is or will remain appropriate.

Every effort has been made to trace all copyright holders, but if any have been overlooked the publisher will be pleased to include any necessary credits in any subsequent reprint or edition.

For further information on Polity, visit our website: politybooks.com

Contents

Timeline of Key Events in AR

December 1945	ENIAC, the first digital computer.
1946–1953	The Macy Conferences on "Cybernetics."
February 1958	The creation, by presidential order, of the Advanced Research Projects Agency of the US Department of Defense (ARPA).
March 1960	J. C. R. Licklider publishes "Man–Computer Symbiosis," a hugely influential work in the field of interactive computing.
December 1962	J. C. R. Licklider appointed to head ARPA's Information Processing Techniques Office (IPTO).
1963	Ivan Sutherland receives his PhD from MIT for his work on Sketchpad.
1964	Sutherland replaces Licklider as head of the IPTO.
1965	Sutherland publishes "The Ultimate Display," the first work to describe an augmented reality.

Timeline of Key Events in AR

December 1968	At the Fall Joint Computer Conference in San Francisco, Douglas Engelbart unveils the groundbreaking, interactive "On-Line System," while Ivan Sutherland reveals his "Sword of Damocles," the first augmented reality system.
1985	The Virtual Interactive Environment Workstation (VIEW), the first modern virtual reality system, is developed at NASA's Ames Research Center.
2001	John Hanke founds Keyhole, purchased by Google in 2004 to serve as the foundation for both Google Earth and Google Maps.
January 2007	Steve Jobs unveils the first smartphone, Apple iPhone.
November 2010	Microsoft introduces the "Kinect" depth camera.
March 2014	Facebook purchases VR startup Oculus for $2 billion.
June 2014	"Cardboard" – a cheap VR platform leveraging the smartphone – introduced at Google I/O's conference.
January 2015	Microsoft introduces "HoloLens," a self-contained augmented reality device.
July 2016	Niantic and Nintendo release *Pokémon Go*, the first augmented reality game played by tens of millions.
November 2017	Apple introduces iPhone X, bringing its integrated "TrueDepth" depth camera to hundreds of millions of smartphones.

Acknowledgments

Augmented Reality had its genesis in Mark Zuckerberg's 2017 F8 keynote, recounted at length in chapter 5. As the implications of Zuckerberg's assertion of Facebook's "right to write" became clearer, together with the first reports of Cambridge Analytica's use of Facebook's data set to manipulate election outcomes, and the reports in *The Australian* about the targeting of emotionally vulnerable teenagers, I formulated a thesis about the shape of things to come. Reaching out to my friend and *Meanjin* editor-in-chief Jonathan Green, he quickly commissioned "The Last Days of Reality" for *Meanjin*'s Summer 2017 issue. That essay represented a first pass at the ideas explored at length in this book, and I am grateful for the opportunity that he provided me.

Although I had given some thought to expanding that title to book length, my efforts proved unsuccessful until I received an unexpected email from Mary Savigar at Polity. Mary would go on to become the commissioning editor for *Augmented Reality*. Although I took my time with the drafting, submission, re-drafting, and

Acknowledgments

resubmission of the proposal for this book, Mary was unfailingly patient, supportive, and insightful; this book owes everything to her persistence.

My friend and colleague in the Media and Communications Department at the University of Sydney, Dr. Fiona Martin, gave me several opportunities to give lectures on the topics explored in this book, helping me to better understand my own themes and how to express them clearly to a lay audience. Fiona was also instrumental in convincing me that this book needed to be written for Polity – and for all of this she has my sincerest gratitude.

Huge appreciation for the folks at Toby's, who kept me well fed and caffeinated during my many breakfast writing sessions.

To everyone else who encouraged, supported, supplied, and refined (you know who you are), my sincerest thanks.

I alone am responsible for any errors that may have found their way into this text.

Introduction:
A Riot in Rhodes

On the evening of July 12, 2016, a large crowd gathered at Peg Paterson Park. Very little distinguishes that park – located in Rhodes, New South Wales – from any of the others threaded among Sydney's vast and growing suburbs. Surrounded on three sides by tall apartment buildings, the park offers a bit of green space and some basic playground facilities, the kind of space ideal for walking the dog – or letting the kids have a bit of well-supervised exercise.

On that evening, the draw for people crowding into Peg Paterson Park had nothing to do with reality. Instead, the virtual world of data and networks had exploded into the physical world of places and people, an eruption that began six days earlier, when a small games company named Niantic released a new smart-phone app.

Niantic's app used the smartphone's camera and other sensors – including Global Positioning System (GPS),

1

which provides accurate coordinates for any location on Earth's surface – mixing all of this input together, adding to it, then displaying that synthesis to the smartphone's screen. The world portrayed on-screen, though rendered in cartoon-like detail, looked similar to the real world, reduced to its essential figures and landmarks. Within this simplified landscape Niantic had situated synthetic, imaginary creatures – *Pokémon*.

Already 20 years old, the *Pokémon* franchise of card and video games, television series, films, books, and comics had revived the fortunes of the once-dominant/ now-struggling video gaming firm Nintendo. The card games became a craze among 8- to 10-year-olds around the world, with sales reaching tens of billions of cards. A whole generation had played *Pokémon*, maintaining a nostalgic love for the imaginary (and cute) monsters.

Niantic's app – *Pokémon Go* – came along at just the right moment to mine that nostalgia within a generation who had come of age in the era of the smartphone. Millennials with the latest iPhone and Android models found *Pokémon Go* drained their smartphone batteries like no app ever had – and turned the real world into the universe of *Pokémon*.

While the card and video games might allow players to imagine another universe where *Pokémon* freely wandered about, *Pokémon Go* united the real world – as sensed by smartphone camera and GPS – with all of the various *Pokémon*, each with their unique look, sound, and capabilities. Within its app, Niantic had lured *Pokémon* out of imagination and into reality.

Introduction: A Riot in Rhodes

Into that newly mixed-up world of real and imaginary, Niantic had added other features, including "Pokéstops" – landmarks keyed to real-world coordinates via GPS, and offering valuable items for the *Pokémon Go* player's inventory – the sorts of tools that would make it easier to catch and train Pokémon.

Wanting to test its new app – and the huge network of cloud-based computers that supported it – Niantic released the app in stages, nation by nation, over a period of months. Australia, as a mid-sized nation with a high rate of smartphone ownership, got it first – and it quickly became a craze. As friend told friend, Australians began to play *Pokémon Go* in vast numbers. Groups of friends struck out together in search of Pokémon and Pokéstops. Hundreds of thousands of players went for a wander around their suburbs, looking for what they might find. For a few days it seemed as though "Gotta Catch 'Em All" had become the national slogan.

As a well-visited landmark in the suburb of Rhodes – mapped out by players of Niantic's other app, *Ingress* – Peg Paterson Park had several Pokéstops. The first folks to stumble upon them told their friends, who told their friends, who told their friends – and those friends shared it on Facebook. All of which meant Peg Paterson Park – conveniently located just a 2-minute stroll from Rhodes' railway station – got very popular, very fast.

Niantic added another clever feature to *Pokémon Go* – lures. Lay down a lure and the chances of attracting a rare and valuable Pokémon increased dramatically. But lures only worked for an hour before they vanished, and – unlike the app itself – lures cost money. Not a lot

3

of money, though – just a dollar. The perfect reason to spend: Make a fun game even more fun.

Players soon learned that lures worked for everyone – not just the player who plumped for the lure. Everyone else around benefited. Drop a lure, and expect to see a few other *Pokémon Go* players turn up – lured in by that lure.

Players at Peg Paterson Park dropped lure after lure – drawing in many rare Pokémon.[1] Players would message other friends – playing somewhere else – telling them to get over to Peg Paterson Park, because it had suddenly become easy to catch rare Pokémon. That combination of Pokéstops and lures, broadcast and amplified by social media, generated a vast crowd – hundreds of players all crowded into a tiny suburban park.

That might have been a matter of little consequence during daytime hours. But as it passed midnight (on a weeknight!), and the crowd showed no signs of dispersing, the police arrived – alerted by noise complaints from the apartment dwellers surrounding the Park,[2] who couldn't get to sleep over the hubbub of happy players. The police ticketed the double-parked cars and asked everyone else to move on – which, eventually, they did.

While players' lures quickly vanished, those Pokéstops remained in Peg Paterson Park – drawing players back again, on successive nights.[3] It never again reached the intensity of that Tuesday evening, but in the aftermath, it became apparent that Niantic had done something unexpectedly potent when it located those Pokéstops in the park, something that perhaps it had not even intended to do. *Pokémon Go* changed players' relationship to space, and changed their behavior within it.

* * *

We've always imagined place: Here a church, there a graveyard, and over there, a school. Each place embodies its own associations, drawn from a mix of culture and memory. What we bring to our experience of place comes from both within and outside of us. While the contents of memory and our mix of emotions vary from moment to moment throughout our lifetimes, the cultural meaning of place tends to be far less mutable. A school means today what it meant yesterday, and will mean much the same tomorrow. Any change in the cultural significance of that place usually occurs so gradually we barely notice it.

While there may be times when a place becomes particularly associated with a cultural moment – such as the World Trade Center – these remain exceptions to a rule: The meaning culture ascribes to place tends to remain as it is. That "inertia," its resistance to change, gives the world a solidity and validity that we rely on. We expect places to be today as they have been in the past.

When a place changes – perhaps a beloved tree has been cut down, or a building burns – we feel something like madness, as our external, collective, and cultural sense of place struggles to adapt to sudden change. Very little can play with our heads as profoundly as place. We take our behavioral cues from place: Sincere in church, somber in the graveyard, open and accepting in school. We "know our place."

Changing place changes us.

With the exception of the theatrical machinery used to entertain and delight – changing place as a way to evoke strong emotions – the ideal of *mutable* place has always been something seen through the mind's eye. We can imagine a place to be transformed, but in reality its inertia keeps it consistent. Or rather, *had* kept it consistent. For although the real will remain stubbornly stable into the foreseeable future, other forces are at work, changing our perception of place – and reality.

Over the last half century, computing has grown progressively more sensual, drawing closer and closer to our bodies. The earliest machines, though physically huge, lacked even the most rudimentary interfaces. Users of these computers "wrote" programs in wiring, physically altering these devices in order to modify their behavior.

The history of computing tells two stories: One, about how these devices became ever smaller and faster; another, about how they became ever more pliable, facile, and responsive. We found it too hard to conform to the ways of the computer, so we shaped these devices to conform to us.

At the mid-point of the twentieth century, computers were a central object of attention – rare, expensive, and demanding. To save money, we learned how to share that massive resource via peripherals – computers accessed via keyboard and screen, then mouse, then touch, becoming more and more natural as the interface moved closer and closer to the body. By the second decade of the twenty-first century, the computer vanished into

We have computers that can now play with our heads, but we have no rules to restrain their engagement.

ubiquity, weaving itself into the fabric of nearly every fabricated object, moving beyond perception.

Just at the moment it disappears from view, computing has acquired the capacity to frame human perception, a figure/ground reversal with enormous consequences. No longer part of the scenery – because it cannot be seen – the computer instead assumes the role of scenery manufacturer, generating reality.

While not wholly creatures of perception, we necessarily observe and respond to our environments. Changes in our environments change us in ways both immediate and permanent.

The computer has now become an actor in the field of reality. In a single step, its capacity to affect us has amplified beyond all expectation – and beyond any frameworks of design, ethics, law, or culture. We have computers that can now play with our heads, but we have no rules to restrain their engagement.

When computers sat comfortably "over there" – visible and therefore limited – we could comprehend and manage their capacities. As they fade into invisibility, with vast new capacities to shape our view of reality, we must consider how we can safely allow them to do so – and how they must announce themselves when doing it.

Something so utterly innocuous as a nostalgic game – capturing fantastical, imaginary Pokémon – can produce unexpected and unprecedented human impacts on the real world. The story of Peg Paterson Park reveals the contours of a future where the blending of the real and the algorithmic could be used – indeed, has already been used – to generate social outcomes.

8

Introduction: A Riot in Rhodes

In itself, this represents nothing new: The dilemma of the Web as information/disinformation medium has created a culture with the greatest population of "disinformed" individuals in human history. Yet the Web occupies (and, it could be argued, pollutes) the internal hyperspace of human thought. It exists within a single dimensionless point, while all the real remains beyond its reach.

Having filled all of the sphere of human thought, the Web now looks to be overtopping its dams, undermining their foundations, and explosively flooding the entirety of the real.[4] The boundary between what we imagine to be true and what can be seen to be true will wash away. *Après moi*, says the Web, *le déluge*.

That flood washes away reality by "augmenting" it at every point. At its most basic level, this new technology of "augmented reality" works like an engine that generates hallucinations – phantasms, projected within the real world. Augmented reality devices make synthetic, "fake" additions to the real world – such as Pokémon sprinkled through a real-world landscape when seen through a smartphone display. Although over half a century old, augmented reality has evolved rapidly over the last several years, and now nears its "unboxing" as a product fit for billions of connected consumers.

This book addresses what the technology of augmented reality does to us, how its use changes us, and how, with some forethought, we can mitigate some of the worst of its effects, perhaps even transforming its impacts. To do that, this book will examine its history, its design, its capacities – and its deep connections to global capital.

9

Introduction: A Riot in Rhodes

A technology freshened up, and presented as "the next big thing" – despite being invented over half a century ago – has rapidly become the *idée fixe* of all five of the world's most technology valuable companies – Apple, Google, Microsoft, Facebook, and Amazon – their Holy Grail. Each has directed billions of dollars toward creating augmented reality systems. What has so ensorceled these giants of rationalism and science into the development of a hallucinogenic medium?

In a word: Control.

Each firm seeks for itself the command over reality, both private and public, that will come from a position with market dominance. Each dreams of translating this command into a vast business empire managing the fabric of the real, a world where corporate and individual world views have been woven together, united by the underlying thread of the new technologies of augmented reality.

The allure of augmented reality will also draw to it actors more powerful than the world's biggest companies. Nations – particularly those with authoritarian aspirations – can and will use augmented reality to manage the behavior of their citizens by changing their relationship to the spaces they move through.

Even if nations somehow avoid this temptation, the fundamental nature of augmented reality means that space will be observed, recorded, quantified, and surveilled as never before. In order to augment a space, its dimensions must be taken. To do this on an ongoing basis, such measurements must be performed continually. To facilitate a world where machines

To facilitate a world where machines and their masters manipulate our reality, we will all be watching one another, all the time, on an unprecedented scale.

and their masters manipulate our reality, we will all be watching one another, all the time, on an unprecedented scale.[5]

This, in brief, characterizes the problem posed by augmented reality.

Against this, we catch glimpses of a great promise – that the "digital depth" pervading our world could be revealed, a world currently hidden from view by these same economic forces and state actors – as a mechanism of control. The real world offers a potential of a universal, revelatory informational transparency, each object illuminated from within by its digitally inscribed meanings.

With that veiling of control laid aside, all of the connections, data flows, and control loops that characterize the made world of the twenty-first century become apparent, substantial, and apprehensible. Visibility – where it can be had, and for as long as it lasts – provides the conditions for addressability, accountability, and awareness. Objects no longer in eclipse can be seen for what they are – and whom they serve. Revelation redistributes power.

The capability to augment reality carries with it a number of key questions: Who ascribes these meanings? Who writes the illuminating scripts? How do they attach themselves to objects in the real? Who gets to overwrite the meanings of the real world? None of this augmentation of reality happens by itself, and all of it forces hard questions, ones that should not be reduced to an ignorant click on a terms-of-service contract. That would transform this redistribution of power into an act of disempowerment.

Introduction: A Riot in Rhodes

Peril undermines promise, just as promise undermines peril.

Much will be promised for the augmentation of reality, but the price remains untabulated. How much would we pay for reality? How much should we be paid to let others drive our view of the real? Can we even frame our experience of the real in transactional terms, or does that indicate the final triumph of Late Capitalism? A reality manipulable by the highest bidder could quickly evolve a license for unlimited, perpetual extraction of our inner lives.

Such fears have old roots, stretching back at least as far as Gutenberg, and have always been both fully justified and entirely overblown. Culture muddles through, walking a tightrope between tyranny and banality, forging a middle path. As Mark Twain purportedly said, the past does not repeat, but it often rhymes.

Yet this moment has its unique qualities. The genius twentieth-century media theorist Marshall McLuhan identified two media that map the place of the body.[6] Architecture situates us within public space, while clothing defines our most personal and private space. We now add a third, augmented reality – both as intensely private as an individual world view, and, because augmented reality systems are always connected, as broadly public as the planetary noosphere. This new hyperconnectivity of place and reality, simultaneously deeply personal, yet thoroughly connected and thereby common, creates a lure to draw us in, like Pokémon at Peg Paterson Park.

Space – and dominion over it, as conferred by the right of title – forms one of the foundations of Law. We use attorneys – rather than armies – to wage wars over each patch of ground, legally arbitrating our spaces and our rights within a space. Changing space changes law, rights, responsibilities, and risks. Our culture of law reflects our spaces, just as our spaces reflect our culture of law. A world with pervasive augmented reality requires new laws, new regulations, new standards – and new behaviors.

Touch reality – or, rather, our perception of the real – and everything within the human sphere bends under that pressure. Innocuous though it may seem to lure and capture cute cartoon monsters via a smartphone app, other monsters from other and far less friendly realms of imagination lie in wait, queued at that same threshold of data and perception, pressure pushing them into the real. We will see the nightmare side of augmented reality, because we cannot experience the benefits without opening ourselves to their opposite.

We cannot know the precise shape of the future. We can look to the past for precedents, and to a present, where, as William Gibson wisely noted, the future already exists – unevenly distributed.[7] At a public park in Rhodes, New South Wales, our augmented reality future began its colonization of the present, landing at Peg Paterson Park and claiming that space as its own, establishing a beachhead of augmentation within the real.

Although it may appear as though the events of that July night had no precedent, the entire arc of computing has led us through an accelerating series of innovations in the relationship between ourselves and our machines, bringing them closer. As they grow closer to us, our machines grow in potency. To understand where we are, and where we are headed, we must begin in chapter 1 by looking back, to our strange eventful history augmenting reality.

The origins of augmented reality (AR) bring us in chapter 2 to a present day of rapid developments in technology – and a battle fought by technology giants to create the first mass-produced AR devices, the so-called "mirrorshades," devices that marry continuous surveillance with an intimate capacity to generate synthetic additions to reality.

Chapter 3 considers how these AR devices might use the information they gather about us, by looking at the whole history of user profiling and user "engagement" – techniques pioneered by Google and Facebook to make content so engaging, so precisely fit to the individual, they find it difficult to look away.

The promise of "digital depth" – the revelation of the inner workings of a deeply technological world largely hidden from view – forms the core of chapter 4. Can we balance the dangers of augmented reality with its enormous potential to liberate and illuminate?

Finally, chapter 5 looks at the ethical questions posed by any attempt to "write" on the world via augmented reality. Who writes, for whom – and who has the "right to write"?

Invented as a machine-amplified empowerment of our native human cognitive and perceptual capacities, augmented reality has evolved into a technology of control. Hence, it is with control we must begin.

1
The Will to Empower

Control has always been at the center of the human relationship to machines.

The steam engine existed as a toy in Alexandrian-era Egypt. Harnessing steam for work proved difficult and dangerous until 1788, when James Watt added a "centrifugal governor," applying the principle of "feedback" to the steam engine, allowing the engine to monitor and regulate its own output. Although the modern steam engine had been invented by Thomas Newcomen three quarters of a century before, Watt's addition of self-regulation saw him credited as the "father" of the steam engine.

Watt's steam engine produced a new tension: As it became possible to build machines vastly more powerful than human beings, it became ever more important to rein in their power. The catalog of the ills of the Industrial Revolution feature many entries that demonstrate the destructive power of machines: Their capacity to rip limbs from bodies, overwhelm their operators, or catastrophically fail to self-regulate – then explode.

In the mid-nineteenth century, James Clerk Maxwell – who gave the world the eponymous equations unifying the electromagnetic forces – wrote an influential paper, *On Governors*, framing the centrifugal governor as a key example of a control system, a system capable of self-regulation.

With the growing capacities of steam-driven machinery – embodied in the locomotive – the idea of control became synonymous with the idea of safety; with the right controls, delivered both automatically and through human oversight (in this case, a locomotive engineer), inhuman forces could be deployed for human benefit.

The word governor has roots that stretch back into Latin – *gubernator* – and further back into Greek – κυβερνήτης – "kubernetes," derived from the word for "steersman," "pilot," or "guide," that is, the person who responds to the boat, the current, and the wind, integrating all of that into subtle shifts and changes in direction. In the 1940s, that governing metaphor of self-control – a pilot guiding a boat through dangerous waters – would find its modern form, in weapons.

A weapon focuses power toward a destructive end, but must not destroy whoever deploys that force, and so exists in that uneasy tension between power and control. Killing power must be balanced rationally, and by design.

In the immediate post-war period, the immense technical advances made by both sides during the conflict slowed and deepened. Although the Messerschmitt jet fighter had been used to great effect by the Luftwaffe, only after the war did aeronautical engineers have the luxury to experiment, expand, and improve on those early efforts. Rapid innovation led to a jet that flew so fast it could approach the speed of sound, with fatal consequences as it encountered its shock wave; or could bank into a turn so rapidly that it slammed the pilot with intense gravitational forces, driving them to unconsciousness as blood pulled away from the brain. The jet fighter had capacities embodied in its design that could prove fatal.

In order to minimize the opportunities for disaster, these early jet fighters crowded their cockpits with an exhaustive array of instrumentation needed for flight, navigation, and combat operations. This stretched the pilot in another direction – toward a condition of "cognitive overload." So much important data, streaming into so many displays, can easily avalanche into confusion. Many pilots tried to master these early jet fighters; only a few had the necessary capacity to safely integrate all of the information they provided, achieving "symbiosis" with the machinery, where aircraft and pilot behaved as a single unit.

That symbiosis of man and machine emerged as one of the central themes of academic discourse in the early post-war era. The "Macy Conferences," gathering the best and brightest from disciplines as diverse as mathematics, neurology, and anthropology,[1] worked toward symbiosis using concepts garnered from both "hard" and "soft" sciences: The 300-year-old Cartesian split between *res cogitans*, our inner life, and *res extensa*, the world of things. Symbiosis, for the Macy conferees, pointed toward a new, active relationship between the inner and outer worlds, one that could be embodied in new kinds of machines.

Each participant, eminent in their own discipline, came with an open mind – and a set of proposals. None came more prepared than Norbert Wiener, a true polymath whose talents extended to mathematics, electronics, systems theory, computing – and a new discipline, which he'd both invented and named after that Greek word for "steersman": *cybernetics.*

Wiener aimed for nothing less than a complete description of the theory of control in *any* system – living or mechanical. Laid out in elegant though nearly inaccessible mathematical detail in his 1948 volume *Cybernetics,*[2] Wiener introduced several concepts that have, in the years since, become so commonplace they seem almost obvious. First among these, feedback: The idea that the output of a process can be used to help control that process. For Wiener, obsessed with the theory of information, this meant *every process generates information that can be used to control it.*

Two years later, in *The Human Use of Human Beings,* Wiener used far more accessible language to explain his cybernetic hypotheses, writing, "Information is the name for the content exchanged with the outer world as we adjust to it, and make our adjustment felt upon it."[3] In this economy of language Wiener unites *res cogitans* with *res extensa* via the exchange of information, describing a system where messages from the world change the internal landscape, while interiority sends messages that change the world, each process informing the other in a dance of feedback.

During the war, Wiener embodied his theories of control and feedback in the design of electronic circuits controlling anti-aircraft guns, allowing them to automatically track their targets. Five months after VJ Day, ENIAC, the first true digital computer, gave mathematicians like Wiener a tool that could "process" information along lines determined by the logic of a "program." Yet, for all its brute force as a numerical calculator, the computer had no significant connections to the outside world, beyond a few switches and relays. All mind and no body, these first computers had *res cogitans* without *res extensa*. They could think, but they could not do, nor could they sense the way their thoughts shaped the world, and respond.

To bridge that divide, the computer would have to become a *cyber-physical* system, a combination of mind plus senses paired with an ability to affect change in the world, then sense those changes. Taking in data continuously generated by a range of sensors, integrating it into an assessment of state, the cyber-physical device could compute decisions that would then be translated into actions. These would in turn generate new sensor data, requiring further integration and assessment, producing still further decisions and actions, generating still more data – on and on and on in a continuous flow, an exchange of content between the outer and inner worlds that seemed to perfectly embody Wiener's conception of cybernetics.

At its essence, a cyber-physical device must be responsive in real time; sensing, deciding, and acting without delay. This real-time operation had not been considered in the design of early digital computers. In

1951, WHIRLWIND, the first computer designed for cyber-physical operations,[4] proved that a computer program could respond in real time to a range of sensor inputs, and, although far too large, heavy, and power hungry to find its way into a jet fighter, WHIRLWIND acted as a key "tool for thinking," a canvas upon which a new generation of computing pioneers could inscribe their own ideas for a symbiosis between a cyber-physical system and a human operator.

Research into "man–computer symbiosis" took a deadly serious turn as the Cold War commenced and development of megaton thermonuclear weapons created the specter of imminent planetary apocalypse. Military commanders needed to operate effectively and accurately within an increasingly narrow window between the launch of a surprise nuclear attack and its culmination. Real-time decision support systems could assist with command and control in these emergency circumstances, demanding the integration and display of vast amounts of often conflicting data, without producing additional cognitive overload among already-stressed decision makers.

The design of such decision support systems owed as much to psychology as to physics or mathematics. At MIT, a post-war center for both computing and sensory psychology, psychologist J. C. R. Licklider consulted on machine-to-human interfaces for SAGE, the Semi-Automatic Ground Environment, a vast continent-wide system designed to provide military decision makers data needed to make decisions about nuclear threats and attacks. SAGE's radar sensors scanned the airspace above and beyond the United States, looking for inbound threats, eventually spanning some 78 early warning "DEW Line" radar stations, networked into a nationwide complex of supercomputers,[5] each staffed with an entire floor of cutting-edge SAGE graphic terminals, where military operators could see, classify, and potentially elevate any perceived threats to their commanders.

Licklider consulted on the design of the SAGE graphic terminals, developing some of the first efforts toward a symbiosis of man and computer, then shared a vision for the possibilities of symbiosis in a brief but hugely influential 1960 paper, "Man–Computer Symbiosis":

> In the anticipated symbiotic partnership, men will set the goals, formulate the hypotheses, determine the criteria, and perform the evaluations. Computing machines will do the routinizable work that must be done to prepare the way for insights and decisions in technical and scientific thinking. Preliminary analyses indicate that the symbiotic partnership will perform intellectual operations much more effectively than man alone can perform them.[6]

These words become the prototype for all of the techspeak over the next half century, as computing, via the man–computer symbiosis, drove huge increases in productivity under the banner of "digitization," as computers took over all of the boring, mechanical work, while humans performed necessary monitoring and decision making. The two sides of the symbiosis entered into an enduring partnership, which Licklider framed perfectly in an operational and business-oriented language that Wiener had never employed.

"Man–Computer Symbiosis" marks the point at which the ideas behind cybernetics, dressed in business clothes, became the aims of the cultural mainstream.

Arguably the foundation of modern computing, Licklider's paper led to his appointment in 1962 as the first director of the Information Processing Techniques Office (IPTO), a tiny department within the massive Advanced Research Projects Agency (ARPA), established in the post-Sputnik panic to close a perceived Cold War "science gap" between the superpowers. The IPTO gave Licklider both a mandate and the budget to resolve some of the larger questions surrounding the design of cyber-physical systems, and their implementations in a richer man–computer symbiosis.[7]

The IPTO performed none of this research itself. Instead, Licklider acted as administrator and cheerleader, dispensing millions of dollars in research grants to university laboratories researching cyber-physical systems. A fair bit of that funding flowed toward MIT's Lincoln Labs, where Licklider funded one researcher specifically focused on the intersection of real-time computing and man–computer symbiosis: Ivan Sutherland.[8]

Although he won a Turing Award – the Nobel Prize of computing – Sutherland has never become a household name like Steve Jobs or Bill Gates, despite the fact that most of their successes built upon Sutherland's foundational work in human–computer interfaces, work that stretches back almost 60 years, to Project Sketchpad. Completed as part of an MIT PhD thesis, Sketchpad provided a visual interface to the computer. Sutherland built upon the various computer display technologies that had been developed during the 1950s to give a computer operator a view – via a cathode ray tube (CRT) screen – onto the computer's operations. Sutherland took the output capability of the display, and added a corresponding input capability, creating the first computer program that could respond to human input in real time.

In this first example of a man–computer symbiosis, a TX-2 computer (a direct descendant of the WHIRLWIND real-time computer) drew its output onto a circular oscilloscope display. At the same time, the TX-2 received input from a "light pen" (much like an electronic stylus you might use on a tablet) held by the Sketchpad user. The user touched the display with the light pen, and as they dragged it across the display, a line appeared. Touch that newly drawn line with the light pen, then drag it across the screen, and the line moved in perfect synchrony with the light pen.[9]

All of that seems quite unremarkable today. It's how computers work. We touch their screens with fingers or mice, draw things, arrange them, copy and paste them, delete or erase them: This is how computers behave when under the control of humans, *because* of Sketchpad. Sutherland's genius reveals itself in the essential simplicity of Sketchpad, in that immediate, one-to-one feedback relationship between human and machine, the very first computational realization of Wiener's description of inner and outer spheres of information, each informing one another. It also informed *all* subsequent human–computer interactions.

Computing as we know it today would be inconceivable without Sketchpad. Everything we do with a

"Man–Computer Symbiosis" marks the point at which the ideas behind cybernetics, dressed in business clothes, became the aims of the cultural mainstream.

screen points back to it. And Sutherland was just getting started.

In 1964, Sutherland, at just 25 years old, assumed the administrator's role at ARPA's IPTO. As Licklider's hand-picked successor, Sutherland continued to fund research driving computing toward an increasingly empowering man–computer symbiosis. Drawing on his own ideas about what that symbiosis might look like, in 1965 Sutherland wrote a brief, clear, and profoundly influential paper titled "The Ultimate Display."[10] Following a brief survey of the possible applications of computer-controlled displays – then both rare and expensive – he concluded with what seemed like a bit of science fiction: A proposal to create a display that provided an ideal symbiosis with a human, so that the display effectively disappears from view:

> The computer can easily sense the positions of almost any of our body muscles. So far only the muscles of the hands and arms have been used for computer control. There is no reason why these should be the only ones, although our dexterity with them is so high that they are a natural choice. Our eye dexterity is very high also. Machines to sense and interpret eye motion data can and will be built. It remains to be seen if we can use a language of glances to control a computer. An interesting experiment will be to make the display presentation depend on where we look ...
>
> With appropriate programming, such a display could literally be the Wonderland into which Alice walked.

Sutherland suggests a man–machine symbiosis so complete that every position and movement of the body can be sensed, computed, and responded to by the machine. And beyond the body, he notes that the motion of the eye can be sensed, and a machine could some day be built to respond to that, as well. When we can do all of that, Sutherland proclaims, we have a display that can behave differently depending on where we look.

Having identified that everywhere-you-look-there-you-are ubiquity as the essential quality of his "ultimate" display, Sutherland landed at Harvard University after finishing up at the IPTO. He started to research exactly what he'd described: A cyber-physical system that put the eye into the display at every point.

How would you do that? Either you'd have to build a completely enveloping display – technically achievable but so expensive as to be entirely impractical – or you could develop a new kind of interface, one that married itself to the human eye in much the same way that Sketchpad's light pen married itself to the hand of the user.

Looking through an eyepiece seemed a straightforward solution. Something like a submarine's periscope, where sensors in the eyepiece would deliver a continuous stream of real-time data on the position and direction of the eyepiece to a computer that would take this information and use it to draw onto the display of the eyepiece. As the eyepiece moved, the computer would be able to change what it drew as it moved, because the computer could sense that movement.

In the mid-1960s, tracking the body (or, in this case, just the eyes) required bulky, heavy, mechanical interfaces – metal struts stretching and releasing tightly coiled springs that altered resistance values within electrical circuits as the eyepiece moved both in position and direction. Those changing values had to be trans-lated from continuous analog voltages into discrete digital data – itself a complex task – then fed into a real-time computer. This stream of information drove a first-of-its-kind computer program that took those values, converted them into representations of the position of the eyepiece and the direction of its gaze, and used that as the fodder for a computer program that drew rudimentary wireframe three-dimensional images onto the eyepiece display.

Sutherland's design revealed just how seamless a man–computer symbiosis could become. Just as Sketchpad harnessed hand–eye coordination to make the interface feel natural and simple (as it still does today when we poke a finger at a smartphone), Sutherland's ultimate display employed the natural and nearly instinctive relationship between eyes, head, and body to craft an illusion of pervasive ubiquity. Wherever you turned your head, or directed your gaze, the eyepiece gave you a view onto an artificial world. The machinery creating that artificial world sensed your position, read the direction of your gaze, and responded by generating the appropriate view.

This eyepiece – together with all of its sensors to measure position and gaze direction – came together in what Sutherland called a "head-mounted display." It featured two eyepieces, one for each eye, with light paths passing through half-silvered mirrors leading to small CRTs, providing a "mixed" view of the real world, plus the synthetic world drawn onto the computer display, paired with a complex mechanical tracking armature, all of it powered by a computer reading the sensor data, and generating real-time three-dimensional computer graphics, drawing that onto the CRT screens. This system of human–sensors–computer–displays defined a new approach to the man–machine symbiosis, far more radical and encompassing than Sketchpad, and much closer to a hypothesized "ultimate display."

Twenty years would pass before Sutherland's raw and brutal technological prototype was given a name beyond the innocuous-sounding "Head-Mounted Display" he assigned it in the title of a landmark 1968 paper[11] describing this foundational cyber-physical system. But the contraption quickly acquired a nickname, drawn from the heavy and somewhat precarious-looking position and eye gaze tracking apparatus supporting the binocular eyepieces and the associated display hardware that hung from the ceiling directly above the person using it: The Sword of Damocles (see figure 1).

Sutherland's Sword of Damocles offered the first taste of an empowering symbiosis between the internal and external worlds of information laid out by Wiener in *The Human Use of Human Beings*. Attention, a product of our internal landscape, determines the position of the head, and direction of our eyes' gaze. The Sword of Damocles measures both, feeding them into a program generating the appropriate informational responses, presenting that information through its eyepieces. A tight feedback loop of information being exchanged between human and computer produced the illusion of an all-encompassing synthetic environment, a fusion of

Figure 1   The Sword of Damocles
Source: The author

the symbolic awareness of the interior world with the computational responsiveness of the exterior world.

Just as Sketchpad defined an enduring model for tactile interactions with computer interfaces, the Sword of Damocles established a template for systems articulating features of Sutherland's "ultimate display." The most immediate descendant of the Sword of Damocles, NASA's Virtual Environment Workstation (VIEW), developed in the mid-1980s, differed from Sutherland's prototype in only one element of design. Like the Sword of Damocles, VIEW employed a head-mounted display, head tracking, and three-dimensional computer graphics – all greatly improved in the years that had elapsed (see figure 2). Unlike the Sword of Damocles, VIEW completely enclosed the human sensorium within a synthetic world entirely of the computer's construction.[12] The Sword of Damocles let people look around the real world, but VIEW created its own virtual environment – a "virtual reality." That term would stick, and become the generic name for all VIEW-like systems that generated the entire synthetic environment from the pitch-black silence of a completely enveloping head-mounted display.

A fully synthetic world made sense for NASA. VIEW would allow Space Shuttle astronauts to rehearse

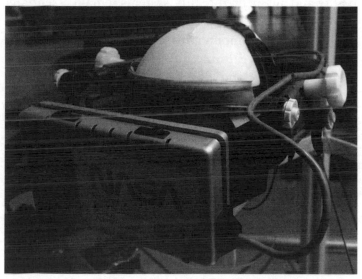

Figure 2 Virtual Environment Workstation (VIEW) head-mounted display by NASA

Source: Sanjay Acharya, via Wikimedia Commons (https://commons.wikimedia.org/wiki/File:Virtual_Reality_Headset_Prototype.jpg)

missions while in-flight and unable to access their extensive ground-based training facilities. That had not been Sutherland's goal with the Sword of Damocles. Its half-silvered mirrors, seamlessly blending the real and synthetic worlds, created a system that was capable of augmenting reality.

Augmented reality predates virtual reality by nearly two decades. It is popularly believed that virtual reality came before augmented reality, largely because it is far easier to create virtual reality than augmented reality. Sutherland solved the hardest problem first, and so comprehensively, that, across more than 50 years of development, the basic elements of all virtual reality and augmented reality systems remain essentially unchanged: A head-mounted display, head tracking, connected to a computer integrating that sensor data, and generating real-time three-dimensional computer graphics. (Sutherland has been reported to be wryly surprised that the state of the art hasn't moved on significantly in all those years.[13])

A reasonable implementation of a fully "immersive," completely synthetic virtual reality system could be constructed from million-dollar graphics supercomputers and first-generation LCD displays available in the mid-1980s. A decade into the microprocessor revolution that would eventually offer nearly inexhaustible computing resources for a few cents, virtual reality could be made workable – but at a high price.

Augmented reality, which calls for an integration between the real and the virtual, taxes sensors and computers well beyond anything required of virtual reality, rendering it tantalizing but largely unachievable, except in one specific circumstance: Attack helicopters. During the mid-1980s, the pilot's helmet in a US Apache attack helicopter got an upgrade, transforming it into an augmented reality display. The Integrated Helmet and Display Sight System (IHADSS)[14] attached an eyepiece to the helmet, giving the pilot control over a thermographic infrared-sensing camera mounted on the front of the helicopter. The camera's orientation mirrored that of the pilot; as the pilot looked around, the camera swiveled on a turret, matching the pilot's gaze direction, a man–computer symbiosis giving the pilot a sensory range extending into the infrared.

Through the 1980s, ARPA's lavish funding continued to drive research and development into four core technologies of augmented reality: Sensing, tracking, displays, and real-time computer graphics. In the early 1990s, the United States realized its post-Cold War "peace dividend," cutting back on military spending, severing the cash lifelines to the giants of the first age of augmented reality – including Ivan Sutherland's pioneering real-time computer graphics firm, Evans & Sutherland. The whole project of man–machine symbiosis, organized around an "ultimate display," entered a downward spiral.

Fortuitously, this happened just as those technologies crossed the barrier from military to civilian use – within the entertainment industry. Sony's 1995 Playstation – the first video game console with real-time three-dimensional computer graphics – ignited a growing trend toward increasing on-screen realism, driving billions of dollars of development toward the mass production of powerful but inexpensive systems. Designed around the constraints of the living room and the family budget, these video game consoles – Playstation and Microsoft's Xbox – soon had hundreds of times the computing power of the NASA VIEW system. Although lacking VIEW's sophisticated sensing of body position and gaze direction, consoles satisfied a generation of gamers with richly detailed three-dimensional virtual environments, managed by complex, button-studded controllers.

In the 20 years between 1995 and 2015, continual improvements under Moore's Law saw computation grow at an exponential rate; overall, computers ran calculations a thousand-fold faster at the end of that interval than at its start. By the mid-2010s, the focus of development dollars and engineering efforts had pivoted away from home entertainment toward personal communications, as embodied by the smartphone.

A powerful yet low-power combination of technologies, the smartphone found an immediate, global audience, with a never-before-seen industrial scale-up of production, quickly running into the billions of units. Commercial competitors seeking to out-do one another on features and performance funded the development of an array of inexpensive new sensors, displays, and real-time computer graphics. Complex electronic components that had cost hundreds or thousands of dollars just a decade before could be purchased for just a few cents by 2015.

With its growth in power and its diverse array of sensors, the smartphone became the stage for a renaissance in augmented reality. Three key technologies removed the roadblocks to realizable augmented reality.

The first of these, Microsoft Kinect, introduced in 2010, straddles the transitional period between video game-driven development and smartphone-driven development of augmented reality.[15] Released as a peripheral for Microsoft's hugely successful Xbox 360 video game console, Kinect used an array of cameras and a patented infrared "dot projection technology" combined with sophisticated computer vision and image-processing capabilities to sense and track objects in the real world, generating a "depth map" – similar to a topographic landscape map – from any scene onto which the user looked.

Although Kinect could quickly capture and map a static environment such as a room (quite a feat in itself), it could also generate a real-time data stream from its continual scans of a dynamic object – such as a person. Using this stream of depth data, Kinect could map human movements onto a synthetic skeleton, reflecting a body's joint movements in space and time, in real time. These movements could then be fed into a video game, allowing a player to use their entire body as the game's controller. Although Kinect represented a vast improvement over mashing buttons on a hand-held controller, as a relatively expensive accessory, Kinect suffered from lackluster sales. Few game developers used Kinect as an interface for their titles, creating a vicious circle that led to the product's eventual withdrawal.

In 2013, Apple – a firm never known for its strength in video games – purchased PrimeSense, the Israeli firm behind Kinect's depth-sensing technology, for US$360 million.[16] Over the course of four years, PrimeSense engineers would miniaturize that technology by a factor of a thousand, until it reappeared as the "notch" on the iPhone X. Apple's "TrueDepth" camera assembly created a depth map from the area in front of the display, providing enough detail to secure its "FaceID" facial recognition software. Apple's massive investment in depth mapping technology had yielded a smartphone sensor capable of accurately mapping space out to a few meters. Although little more than an expensive after-thought for video gaming, depth mapping became a key enabling technology for the smartphone.

The second key technology for augmented reality also had its roots in the pre-smartphone era. In 2001, John Hanke, a video game entrepreneur, founded Keyhole, a geospatial data visualization firm blending real-time three-dimensional computer graphics with big data sets – combining satellite photography, topographical, economic, and political information about everywhere on the Earth's surface. Keyhole generated a near-photorealistic model of the world, based on the best available data.

The world-as-model implemented by Hanke's Keyhole had its genesis in the 1960s, with R. Buckminster Fuller's "World Game." A vast, complex computer simulation – data-driven, digitized, but not visualized – World Game offered a tantalizing capability: Set and read all of the inputs and outputs on "Spaceship Earth."[17] Fuller prophesied a representation of the world as a system understood through informational interactions – just as Wiener might have wanted – 40 years before Keyhole tied all of its elements together into a single tool.

CNN used Keyhole extensively during their rolling coverage of the 2003 war in Iraq, and that garnered the attention of search giant Google. Aware that many of the users of their search engine sought not text, but proximity – wanting to find something near them – Google saw in Keyhole a solution to that problem, and, in 2004, acquired Hanke's startup,[18] integrated its data set into their search engine, and wrapped a new interface around it, creating a combination so potent that when Steve Jobs introduced iPhone to the world in January 2007, he highlighted one app in particular: Google Maps.

A powerful, handheld computer with touch interface, plus graphical display, plus mobile broadband, plus global positioning system (GPS) allowed Google Maps on iPhone to access and display the Keyhole-Google data set. Together with the Mobile Safari web browser, Google Maps made the iPhone a "must-have" device, delivering a location-aware map to the palm of the hand, backed up by an Internet of informational resources. The "hybrid energy"[19] released through the fusion of location and data drove the smartphone to become the fastest-selling tool in history.

Following his success with Google Maps, Hanke put together a working group within Google to work on location-based gaming. Dubbed Niantic Labs, his team worked to blend Google's ever-expanding real-world data set with a synthetic – and imaginary – layer of gaming data.[20] That data told a fictional backstory: Exotic matter, accidentally created by CERN's particle accelerator, and a battle over how its new power would be used – or withheld.

Released at the end of 2013, Niantic's location-aware game – *Ingress* – pitted players around the world, arrayed on one of two teams, in "capture the flag" contests for control of sites around prominent features in the real-world landscape, such as public art, landmarks, and so forth. Marrying the world of places and things (located via GPS) with an invisible world of teams and conspiracies gave *Ingress* a unique flavor, telling a tale hidden in plain sight, invisible to all but those playing the game, overwriting the landscape of the real world with another layer of meaning.

Google spun out Niantic as an independent company in 2015. Hanke and his engineers had already taken the lessons learned from *Ingress* and applied them to their next game, one that would land with such spectacularly unexpected and riotous results in July of 2016: *Pokémon Go*. Using the smartphone camera to map the landscape and populate it with Pokémon, Niantic had perfected a blend of real and imaginary, making it a massive international success, introducing millions of players to the playful potential of augmented reality.

The third and final of the three enabling technologies for augmented reality arrived on June 25, 2014, when David Coz and Damien Henry, engineers working for the Google Cultural Institute in Paris, came to the podium at Google I/O, the firm's annual conference for engineers and developers of Google products. They showed how they'd fashioned a simple framework for a smartphone using the thick, reinforced cardboard from a pizza box, adding two holes to hold a pair of cheap plastic lenses, mounting these eyepieces into the framework directly in front of the smartphone's display. It all looked a bit like a cheap set of binoculars, aimed not at the world, but at the smartphone's screen.

An application written by the pair divided the smartphone display into separate right and left windows, each showing the same scene, but from a slightly different point of view, in a technique known as "binocular stereo," a feature of three-dimensional displays going all the way back to the original Sword of Damocles (and, before that, to the ViewMaster and early stereo photography). Put your eyes up to the plastic lenses and – *voila!* – Coz and Henry had transformed a smartphone into a virtual reality system.[21]

More than just a head-mounted display, this aptly-named "Google Cardboard" repurposed the onboard accelerometer normally used to flip the orientation of the smartphone display between portrait (long) and landscape (wide) modes, using it and the smartphone's onboard compass to track the rotation of the head in space. The smartphone already had everything it needed to track the orientation of the head, plus it offered massive computing power within its few hundred grams, with more than enough capacity to draw complex three-dimensional images to the high-resolution display. Tracking, display, and real-time computer graphics, the three key elements of the Sword of Damocles, could be found on a device that cost a few hundred dollars – and had already been manufactured in the hundreds of millions.

When Coz and Henry mounted the stage at Google I/O, the number of virtual reality systems in the entire world came to no more than a few thousand. An hour later, the number of virtual reality systems had increased by at least ten-thousand-fold. Nearly every reasonably modern smartphone (by 2014 standards) could handle the tracking, display, and real-time computational requirements to create virtual reality. As the barrier to adoption of virtual reality evaporated, a field long thought to be dead (or no more than a punchline) suddenly roared back to life. A new generation of virtual reality systems came to market over the next two years, each looking much like the rearranged internal components of a smartphone, with sensors sourced from smartphone component vendors, and displays sourced from the same manufacturers, together with the welcome addition of real-time computer graphics systems repurposed from high-end video gaming systems.[22] A standalone virtual reality system that would have cost half a million dollars in the early 2010s could be had for a thousandth of that price just a few years later. In the space of months, virtual reality had gone from difficult and expensive to commonplace and cheap.

Although synthetic worlds have become commonplace, integrating those worlds into the real world – the essence of augmented reality – requires another immense technological leap. Virtual reality tracks the position and orientation of the head (and often the hands). Virtual reality knows nothing about nor needs to know about the world beyond its synthetic imagination, crafting a private universe. So private, in fact, that bringing more than one person into a "shared" virtual world has proven difficult. The difficulty has little to do with the technology, but, rather, lies in a fact revealed by virtual reality: Our bodies encode and present so much of our tacit knowledge of space that, removed from space, they become nearly impossible to represent.

Augmented reality keeps the bodies of its users (and all bodies) within this world. To do that requires precise, detailed, and continuously updated measurements of the world.

Fundamentally anchored to the real world, augmented reality keeps the bodies of its users (and all bodies) within this world. To do that requires precise, detailed, and continuously updated measurements of the world. Sutherland's Sword of Damocles used half-silvered mirrors to bring the world to the eyepiece, mixing the synthetic with the real, but no technology available in the 1960s could have captured the device's operating environment – or the body operating it – in any detail. Sutherland described his "Ultimate Display" as *Alice's Adventures in Wonderland*, but could only deliver *Flatland*.

When the three key technologies of depth mapping, geospatial data sets, and inexpensive but powerful hardware came together in the second half of the 2010s, it became possible to design fully featured augmented reality tools. An enveloping man–machine symbiosis, first described in mathematical terms by Wiener, then as a form of human empowerment by J. C. R. Licklider, and implemented in its foundational elements by Ivan Sutherland in both Sketchpad and the Sword of Damocles, finally came together in the first fully realized augmented reality system: Microsoft's *HoloLens*.

It had taken nearly 50 years to make augmented reality real.

2

Surveillance Status

The tradition of "magical" technology demos stretches all the way back to December 9, 1968, when an engineer and visionary named Douglas Engelbart took to an auditorium stage before a standing-room-only crowd at the Fall Joint Computer Conference in San Francisco. Over the course of 90 minutes Engelbart demonstrated the future of the man–computer symbiosis via a projected wall-sized image of his head, displayed next to a wall-sized projection of the computer screen he manipulated, showing attendees what it meant to "augment human intellect."

What Engelbart meant by such high-flung language seemed simple enough: Cutting and pasting text, moving them around with a few clicks of a mouse, linking the contents of one file with another, and videoconferencing with a colleague some 30 miles away. None of this feels at all foreign to anyone working with a computer in the twenty-first century, but this was the first time that

43

any of these things had been demonstrated publicly. Copy-and-paste? Engelbart invented it. The mouse? Invented that, too. Linking files together? Yes; here are the first fledgling steps toward the World Wide Web. And videoconferencing – billions of us do this all the time with our smartphones when we Zoom or Skype.

In his "Mother of All Demos," as it became known, Engelbart presented a complete, coherent, and wholly defining future for computing: A world where these massive, expensive, and difficult machines had become small, manageable, and personal.[1] Although it took the world the better part of a generation to catch up with Engelbart (true to his cantankerous nature, he was never really satisfied with anyone else's attempts to improve on his early efforts), nearly every element we think of as central to "modern" computing had its roots in the Demo. The Demo also established a precedent: Every subsequent Great Leap Forward in computing would strive for this same feeling of magic so potent it could change the world.

When Steve Jobs demoed the Apple Macintosh in 1984, or his NeXT workstation in 1988, or the iPod in 2003, each of his reveals cribbed from the theatrical playbook laid down by Engelbart and that Mother of All Demos. The most famous of those reveals arrived unexpectedly in 2007, when from the Macworld stage Jobs famously said, "One more thing ...," then spent 90 minutes demonstrating Apple's iPhone.

In a half century following the Mother of All Demos, many technology companies have tried to harness this magic. Nearly all have failed. Perhaps once in a decade a world-changing product emerges from the fanfare, something that changes everything: Apple's Macintosh in the 1980s, iPhone in the 2000s – and, on January 21, 2015, Microsoft's HoloLens.[2]

That morning, in a Seattle auditorium, a crowd waited patiently for the ho-hum release of Windows 10 Home, the consumer edition of Microsoft's latest-and-best computer operating system. Then – almost miraculously – the software giant found its own "One more thing ..." moment, as "Chief Inventor" Alex Kipman took to the stage, revealing something no one in the technology world had expected (and certainly not from a stodgy business software firm): A fully realized, standalone augmented reality headset.

It was as if Bill Gates had shown up in a flying saucer.

Yet none of this should have come as a surprise. Microsoft had invested heavily in the engineering talent and enabling technologies behind HoloLens. In the early 1990s, realizing that home computers running their Windows operating system did dual duty as video game machines, Microsoft began a long-term commitment to real-time 3D computer graphics, working closely with both game studios and hardware manufacturers to ensure that computers running its operating systems always delivered the highest possible performance.

In 1999, the firm took that a step further, manufacturing their own PC – but one disguised and sold as a video game console.[3] Stripping away all the elements unnecessary for entertainment, Microsoft's Xbox used the high-performance software and hardware as found on home PCs – and played the same games, quickly becoming the dominant video game console, stealing the crown from Sony's Playstation.

45

In late 2003, Sony introduced a revolutionary new accessory for its high-powered Playstation 2.[4] Via an inexpensive "webcam," Sony's EyeToy streamed video into the console, where state-of-the-art image recognition software detected shapes, such as hands and fingers. EyeToy transformed players' fingers into the equivalent of video-game controllers, allowing them to draw beautiful patterns on the display simply by moving fingers in front of the camera, taking Sutherland's work with Sketchpad to its logical conclusion, replacing light pen and screen with hands and camera.

In response to the competitive threat posed by the wildly popular EyeToy, Microsoft launched "Project Natal" – later renamed Kinect – a depth camera creating a three-dimensional map of the world as seen through its three-camera array. Mounted on a fixed point (generally above or below the display), Kinect took in a fixed view of the world, while players moved in front of it. As with EyeToy, Kinect translated human movements into a stream of data that could control a game – but with far greater precision.

A tiny and obvious change transformed the Kinect from game accessory to enabling technology for the augmented reality HoloLens: Rather than attaching the device to a fixed point, where it would scan the same environment repeatedly, why not attach it to a person? Mounted to a human body, the depth camera would be able to scan the whole environment as the person moved through it. Reversing the electronic gaze of Kinect allowed HoloLens to generate one of the fundamental requirements for augmented reality – a richly detailed map of the environment.

Wherever it operates, augmented reality relies on a precise, particular, and complete map of the real world. This map supports the essential illusion of augmented reality – a seamless blending of real and imaginary worlds. Although in certain rare cases, such maps can be generated in advance – allowing that nothing within that map moves, ever – in nearly every imaginable instance this map (or at least a fair portion of it) must be created in real time from sensors such as depth cameras.

Kinect's 30 cm-wide depth camera shrank in HoloLens to a pair of sensors small enough to be mounted within a band that runs around the head and looks a lot like a futuristic industrial safety visor (see figure 3). HoloLens emphasizes its connection to reality through both its see-through eyepiece displays (just like the original Sword of Damocles) and its multiple, outward-facing sensors. Instead of using a bulky and limiting armature to track the head, HoloLens uses its head-mounted sensors to track the world as the device moves through it.

The honey-I-shrunk-the-Kinects embedded within HoloLens provide real-time sensor data. Translating that data into a meaningful map requires a very sophisti-cated bit of software known as SLAM – or Simultaneous Localization and Mapping.[5]

This problem of real-time mapping has application far beyond augmented reality; autonomous vehicles may have a complete map of the road system, yet still need a continuous stream of sensor data to help them avoid obstacles and accommodate all the changing features of the real world. A static map, while helpful,

Figure 3 Microsoft HoloLens, with cameras used for SLAM
Source: Ramadhanakbr, via Wikimedia Commons (https://commons.
wikimedia.org/wiki/File:Ramahololens.jpg)

can never cover all conceivable cases. Similarly, when a domestic robot such as a Roomba vacuums its way through a home, it builds a map of the contours of the floor from the sensor data it receives as it moves, but even with that map in its memory, it still needs real-time sensor data to avoid vacuuming the cat.

HoloLens uses its depth cameras to build a dynamic map of the world around it, with its sensors streaming their depth data into the HoloLens software, which then calculates the location of the HoloLens within space, while *simultaneously* using that data to develop a detailed three-dimensional map of the space.

That's a difficult task – as if a smartphone mapping app (like Google Maps) knew nothing about the world when launched, being forced to learn everything about the world within a space of a few seconds, by scanning the local road network, using that scan to create a map, then dropping a pin onto that map to signify your precise location. Mapping apps never work that way

– it's far more efficient to feed GPS location information to a geographical data set – such as Keyhole. To do both localization and mapping together, as HoloLens does, requires a lot of computer power, and fast, light, high-quality sensors.

In addition, the full localization-and-mapping process has to happen quickly enough within HoloLens that a user never becomes impatient, waiting for the scan to complete its creation of a map of the world. HoloLens cleverly divides the SLAM process into two complementary components: A first-pass scan of a space that detects the fixed contours, such as walls and immoveable furniture – equivalent to the "road map." In that first pass, HoloLens asks a user to look about, while its depth cameras measure the dimensions of the space, simultaneously creating a simplified "fingerprint" of the space. The next time a user dons a HoloLens within that space, a momentary scan resolves the "fingerprint" of the space, and HoloLens uses that fingerprint to retrieve the full scan.[6]

During the second phase of the SLAM process, HoloLens detects dynamic features – moveable furnishings and people. When added into the map built up during the first scan, HoloLens has the data it needs to augment the real-world environment with synthetic creations. Those augmentations come in the form of faux "holograms." Although Microsoft appropriated the language of optics and laser physics, these "holograms" have nothing in common with real holograms. Instead, HoloLens uses its SLAM-generated data set to place synthetic objects within the environment with absolute positioning. Ghostly, glowing, and semi-transparent, these "holograms" have a three-dimensional quality: They occupy space, and can be examined from any position or angle, even (where the feature has been implemented) "poked" by a HoloLens user's hand.

Making these faux holograms visible required another enabling technology. Where the Sword of Damocles used half-silvered mirrors to mix the real-world with synthetic images, HoloLens uses a "waveguide" lens to optically pipe computer-generated images into the eyepiece – a series of displays sandwiched between layers of glass, creating a very thick lens. Drawn across several of the display layers, images appear as if projected from within the lens itself, doing so without blocking any of the light coming through the lens from the outside world. The effect feels almost magical – as if a glowing, illuminated object has appeared within the glass. Drawn and re-drawn 30 times a second – to reflect changes as the user's head moves around – it creates the illusion of three-dimensional solidity.

Microsoft squeezed all of this exotic technology – plus a hefty battery – into a visor small enough and light enough that, if not exactly comfortable, could be worn and used for an hour or more. A marvel of miniaturization and usability, HoloLens demonstrated that Sutherland's "Alice in Wonderland" vision of the "Ultimate Display" could be made real – and, more importantly, manufacturable: The prototype Microsoft revealed was no pie-in-the-sky technology concept, nor a ramshackle prototype, but an early production run of the version they began selling to a curious public a year later.

Although hardly cheap – Microsoft charged US$3,000 for the headset – nothing like HoloLens had ever been seen before. A year and a half before *Pokémon Go* landed on smartphones, Microsoft's HoloLens became the category-defining example of augmented reality. Everything afterward that purported to be augmented reality would be measured against what HoloLens had already achieved.

Yet as a first-of-its-kind device, HoloLens also had its share of drawbacks and compromises. Beyond its bulk, weight, and relatively short battery life, almost every user immediately experienced the frustration of a tiny field of view. The waveguide optics in HoloLens covered only a small portion of the area that the eye takes in – the full human field of view spans about 135 degrees, horizontally, where HoloLens, at best, offered 40. Outside that narrow window, the images generated by HoloLens disappeared. This made the user feel as though the augmented world lay on the other side of a narrow porthole, forcing them to move their heads in, out, and around, as they tried to grasp a complete view of their augmented environment. That porthole view broke the illusion of the seamless integration of the real and synthetic worlds,[7] while simultaneously highlighting the impressive SLAM capabilities of the device: Turn away, move around, even leave the space altogether, yet upon return everything would appear exactly where it had been placed.

Through its fingerprinting of spaces, HoloLens builds up a detailed data set about all the places where it gets used, data stored on the device[8] and in Microsoft's Azure cloud computing infrastructure. Although entirely effective as an augmented reality system, HoloLens does not attempt to do everything by itself – nor could it. The device benefits greatly from a continuous connection to a rich set of spatial computing cloud services. Spatial fingerprints can be stored into the cloud, along with the spatial coordinates of holograms and other features. A user can pick up a HoloLens they've never used before, log into it, and use it to access all of their previously scanned spaces from Microsoft's cloud. With cloud connectivity, the content of an augmented reality can be completely divorced from any device generating a view of it.

This represents sound engineering practice – similar to the way that the content of a Web page remains separate from a Web browser – but produces a significant and underappreciated side effect: *By design, augmented reality is a technology of networked surveillance.*

Pokémon Go uses the smartphone's camera plus GPS plus an accelerometer plus a compass to determine the player's view into its augmented reality world. This means that while playing the game, the *Pokémon Go* player has all those sensors – and in particular, their smartphone camera – continuously engaged, always recording. In order to maintain the spatial awareness integral to the game, the smartphone has been turned into a surveillance device. Threaded into the essence of the game, this surveillance seems not only condign, but welcome. Launch the game and the smartphone turns itself into a device that intensively gathers data from all appropriate sensors to locate and orient the device with enough precision that it can be used to convincingly open a portal into a synthetic world.

Despite this obvious transformation of their smart-phones into the machinery of surveillance, *Pokémon Go*

By design, augmented reality
is a technology of networked
surveillance.

players only noted (and complained about) the energy consumed by the game. Interpreting a real-time stream of data from multiple sensors to generate SLAM, plus integration of that data, monopolized the smartphone's processor.[9] Moreover, maintaining a player's view onto the synthetic world of Pokémon meant the display kept glowing, all the time. Surveillance comes with a high power budget: An average smartphone can go from fully charged to empty within an hour of launching *Pokémon Go*. As the game frequently invites players on long exploratory journeys, dedicated players stock up on external batteries and charging cables to keep their smartphone well supplied with power.

While the smartphone performs SLAM and generates the view into the game's synthetic world, players rely on network services (a more polite term than "surveillance") residing in Niantic's cloud to populate the game with creatures and features. Remove a smartphone from its connections (by putting it into "Airplane Mode"), and without its tether to cloud-based resources, it cannot even launch *Pokémon Go*. The game does not really reside on the smartphone; the smartphone acts simply as an interface through which players can interact with Niantic's cloud-based augmented reality services – via that continuous surveillance – services developed for its first augmented reality game, *Ingress*.

Starting with Google's data set of maps – obtained via its acquisition of Keyhole – Niantic used those maps to build *Ingress'* game world and situate its "portals." Those portals established the initial state of the game. However, as an augmented reality app – one that continuously read sensor data, integrating that data into the game, and sending a stream of that data back to Niantic's servers – game play deepened the locative data set available to Niantic.

Like ants laying down a scent trail for other ants to follow, *Ingress* players gathered data on the real world through their play activities, sending that data back to Niantic, adding to Niantic's data set of the world, and enriching the texture of *Ingress* game play.[10] As players explored the real world, their explorations became game content – and a goldmine for Niantic. Every map always differs significantly from the territory it represents, so the difference between the Google data set and the surveillance data gathered by *Ingress* players represented a significant improvement and detailing of that data set. Niantic found a way to dramatically multiply the value of Google's data – and did so using labor given freely by *Ingress* players,[11] just as Facebook's users freely provide valuable updates and photos to a trillion-dollar company.

Feeding the results of surveillance back into the surveillance system dramatically improved the accuracy of Niantic's world model, giving it the data resources needed to build a *Pokémon Go* title that would be both usable and richly detailed before anyone had played the game, because it leveraged all of the surveillance data gathered by *Ingress* players.

As a next-generation augmented reality title, *Pokémon Go* used a continuous stream of data from the smartphone camera – in addition to the smartphone's GPS, accelerometer, and compass – to fully integrate the real world with the synthetic world. But because the game continuously used the camera, *Pokémon Go* provided something that *Ingress* could not – live and extensive video coverage from every one of the millions of its players.

That video coverage, integrated with all the other sensor data gathered by the *Pokémon Go* app, provides everything needed to generate detailed and fully three-dimensional models of any place – via a sophisticated computer algorithm known as "photogrammetry." Players, moving through a location like Rhode's Peg Paterson Park (as described in the Introduction), generate an exquisitely rich map of the territory, just through their normal game-playing activities.

Google relies on vehicles to scan and record details of roads and urban landscapes for Google Maps; Niantic merely harnessed human playfulness and our competitive instincts, turning each *Pokémon Go* player into unwitting surveillance-gathering drone. Given the game's immense popularity, Niantic quickly gathered possibly the most detailed global map ever created. Although it does not cover every square meter of the planet, Niantic's player-generated mappings offer incredible detail in those areas most frequently trafficked by – and therefore most interesting to – other human beings.

Although many complain about Google's more obvious urban data harvesting – its mapping cars serving as visible reminders of that harvesting – few have noted that Niantic captured far more detailed data on a far greater scale than anything ever attempted by Google, and did so at nearly zero cost to themselves. In one of its most paradoxical qualities, as a technology built on networked surveillance, augmented reality tends to make that surveillance a seamless part of the experience

– and thereby makes it invisible. With *Pokémon Go*, as with *Ingress* before it, users don't notice the surveillance, enthralled by the game play.

Microsoft's HoloLens, a dedicated device for augmented reality, occupies an ambiguous position, neither hiding its inherent qualities as a surveillance system (studded with cameras, that would prove difficult) nor doing anything to highlight them. This contrasts markedly with the design of the earlier and far less sophisticated Google Glass: Also equipped with a camera, Glass lit a red LED when the device entered its video capture mode. The presence of that LED alerted anyone near the Glass wearer that they were (potentially) under surveillance, something that reportedly produced some sudden ejections from establishments where the patrons objected to being recorded, and leading to the wearers of the devices being tarred with the epithet "Glassholes."[12]

That strong reaction to the surveillance capacities of Google Glass appears to be reflected in the design of HoloLens. While the HoloLens cameras can clearly be seen, they're placed behind curvaceous plexiglass paneling, inset just enough to seem not quite as menacing as a front-mounted, forward-facing camera, such as that found on Google Glass. This allows anyone within proximity to the HoloLens to easily ignore the cameras, depth sensors, and microphones, even though they are nearly always active. Everything about the physical design of HoloLens de-emphasizes its essential function as a head-mounted sensor rig, one that employs multiple sensors to perform SLAM, map space, and mix the synthetic with the real.

If Microsoft had designed HoloLens to alert others to its array of active, recording sensors, it would glow alarmingly, implicitly warning people to stay away from its users, and achieving the opposite of its desired effect: To seamlessly integrate the synthetic with the real world, in both its physical and relational aspects. Instead, HoloLens records actively but silently, a forest of half-hidden cameras necessary to generate its perceptual illusions.

This hiding of surveillance in plain sight mirrors the way millions of CCTV cameras have been deployed in urban environments to manage crime – or, in the case of China, a restive population. The visible presence of the surveillance device changes the behaviors of those observed by it.

The first edition of HoloLens, released in 2016, sold only a few tens of thousands of units. The second edition HoloLens 2, introduced three years later, featured a wider field of view, and looks to be on a similar sales trajectory. A few more surveillance devices add up to a drop in the ocean when measured against the millions of surveillance systems installed worldwide, or the billions of smartphones now capable, via AR apps like *Pokémon Go*, of transforming themselves into networked surveillance systems.

As an initial implementation of an augmented reality device, Microsoft's first HoloLens will likely be remembered with fondness, much like those "brick" analog cellular phones used by businesspeople in the mid-1980s – an early, clumsy example of a technology that quickly became small, light, and ubiquitous. The concept of "mirrorshades"[13] – high-quality augmented reality displays no bulkier or heavier than a pair of sunglasses – has been a trope of cyberpunk science fiction since the late 1970s. People instinctively gravitate toward the idea of mirrorshades displays – both because sunglasses convey a cool, psychological distance, and because they imply both style and comfort.

Back in 2017, Facebook founder and CEO Mark Zuckerberg discussed the future of augmented reality efforts at the social media giant, showing a slide of a pair of mirrorshades – with a synthetic world photoshopped into the lenses. But he also acknowledged the technical difficulties involved in creating them:

> I think everyone would basically agree that we do not have the science or technology today to build the AR glasses that we want. We may in five years, or seven years, or something like that. But we're not likely to be able to deliver the experience that we want right now.[14]

Zuckerberg could not deliver Facebook mirrorshades in 2017, nor did he believe it likely to happen until the middle years of the following decade. But along with almost every other person deeply immersed in the field, he believes that mirrorshades will exist, and will come to market by the middle of the 2020s.[15] Apple, long rumored to be working on their own design, will likely use its iPhone as the brains of its AR mirrorshades, keeping the displays themselves light and comfortable.[16] Facebook will likely use its Oculus division to design its own hardware. Similar projects have been reported at Google and Amazon, while Microsoft continues to refine HoloLens. At one point or another, all or most of the American tech giants have made research efforts toward the development of mirrorshades AR – along with Samsung, Huawei, and Chinese smartphone giant Oppo.[17]

With trillions of dollars of available capital focused on the solution of what remains a substantial engineering and manufacturing problem, AR mirrorshades seem to be inevitable. Sometime in the 2020s we can expect them to roll off assembly lines in the tens, and then hundreds of millions of units – a scaling similar to that of the smartphone a decade earlier.

At that point, the surveillance status intentionally downplayed in the design of HoloLens will become impossible to ignore – or escape. When hundreds of millions of people don AR mirrorshades, each of them actively sensing, analyzing and integrating data from the world around them, *we will unintentionally co-create a world where we have each placed one another under the tightest surveillance in human history.*

None of the users of these AR mirrorshades will be aware that they're wearing surveillance devices. The failure of Google Glass, when measured against the success of HoloLens – designing a device for surveillance that produces no reaction to it – guarantees that these devices will do everything in their power to render their essential surveillance function as invisible and inaccessible as possible. Yet these devices must be designed as networked surveillance systems, continuously streaming real-time sensor data into the cloud for analysis, processing, and storage. Just as websites such as Facebook carefully monitor and record all of the user behavior on those sites (and through the use of tracking

These devices will do everything in their power to render their essential surveillance function as invisible and inaccessible as possible.

"cookies," well beyond those sites), these AR devices will vacuum up as much user data as the device can upload to the network.

Just as Niantic used *Ingress* and *Pokémon Go* to grow vast sets of geolocational data, each of the manufacturers of these AR systems will design them to gather data about their users: Their comings and goings, their associations, and their activities. All of that information will feed into systems generating increasingly rich and accurate user profiles – something Facebook has already been doing with its Web users since the early 2010s. But AR systems provide far more detailed data, accurately documenting every moment, via cameras, depth sensors, microphones, GPS, and an array of other sensors.

Before gathering this treasure trove of profiling data – freely and unwittingly offered up by AR mirrorshades owners – the companies purveying these devices will need to persuade a tech-overwhelmed polity that augmented reality offers a real solution to a problem – without revealing that problem as something these companies created.

3
The Last Days of Reality

"Sorry."

People look up from their screens, see the situation they've walked into – unaware – and reflexively apologize.

It happens everywhere. Parents pushing strollers. Pedestrians strolling across busy intersections. Kids standing in the middle of the sidewalk. Every one of them transfixed by a screen, more absorbed in the play of light than in the world around them. Even toddlers, barely out of the crib, have learned how to hold a tablet between their hands as their parents, similarly preoccupied with their smaller screens, push them about.

We seem to have lost any capacity to resist the lure of the screen. Yet before the smartphone we had few such issues. Mobile phones – nearly as popular then as today – consumed a far smaller part of our sensory experience. Something changed with the arrival of the smartphone, both within the device, and, a few years later, with our relation to that device. The smartphone has changed, and changed us.

When Steve Jobs walked onto the stage at San Francisco's Moscone Center, back in January 2007, with "One more thing ..." in his hand, he knew Apple had distilled into its design everything learned over a quarter of a century of experimenting with human–computer interfaces (HCI). The way iPhone responded visually, in response to tactile input, produced a sense of delight and wonder in its users. For those users, that something so compact could be so responsive felt nearly magical.

To create that magic, Apple pushed existing technologies to their limits, crafting an energy-hungry gadget which couldn't even survive a day of moderately active use without needing a recharge. Senior management at Nokia and Microsoft – Apple's competitors in the market for high-end mobiles – saw this as the iPhone's Achille's heel, and predicted its rapid demise. Instead, in an unprecedented transformation of user behavior, iPhone owners found ways to keep the device charged. The portmanteau "powerwhoring" entered the English language, as users looked for available outlets in airports, cafés, hotel lobbies – anywhere they could plug in the device's charger for a few minutes.

This misapprehension of the almost magnetic lure of iPhone spelled doom for Nokia. Although its market capitalization in 2007 equaled all of the rest of the companies listed on the Helsinki stock exchange, within a decade, Nokia would be sold off at a fire-sale price to Microsoft, part of the software giant's own efforts to rescue its imploding mobile market share against the dominance of the iPhone.[1]

This unprecedented and unpredicted industrial collapse pointed toward an unrecognized element in Apple's new smartphone – that this sense of wonder and delight produced and continuously reinforced a strongly positive feeling toward the device. People didn't just use the iPhone – they loved it. The sight of long queues waiting outside an Apple Store to purchase the latest model of iPhone became part of the landscape, expected with every new release. The device inspired both immense brand loyalty and a relationship unlike that produced by any other technological artifact, other than the automobile.

Where the automobile signified freedom and identity, the smartphone pointed inward, toward a world of connectivity, attachment, and relation. Yet each built their intimate relationships with their users upon their performance. The thrill of acceleration at the touch of a pedal and the magical delight at the tap of a finger both leave an impression upon our interior landscapes. They flood us with good feelings, and those feelings leave a residue in our behavior. As a result, for nearly a century we have inhabited a culture shaped by the presence of the automobile, and – since the late 2000s – similarly shaped by the smartphone.

Only a very few technological artifacts have this unique, almost gravitational, quality, capable of warping the fabric of culture. Among the countless innovations of the last 500 years of human culture, only a handful have fundamentally reshaped the world: The printing press, telegraph, motion picture, radio, television, and World Wide Web.

Within a decade of its introduction, nearly half of all people alive – and a clear majority of those over

18 years old – owned a smartphone.[2] No other tool has ever charted a path from invention to ubiquity in such a compressed time span. The smartphone, in this sense, possesses a unique and almost magical quality, seemingly casting a "glamour" over the whole of the human race, making itself absolutely irresistible.

For much of the developing world, that glamour has the color of money. The connectivity of the smartphone – and the mobile, before it – allows individuals to earn more. The device quickly pays for itself with the opportunities it provides.[3] For these billions, the smartphone means more income, a transactional relationship that grows stronger with every opportunity.

Conversely, for the billion living in developed economies, the popularity of the smartphone has very little to do with its potential as an economic amplifier. Instead, the relationship seems to be much more primal, with an emotional, even relational, tone: People seem to have fallen in love with their smartphones.

The roots of this intense relationship to an electronic device stretch back to the early 1960s, with Ivan Sutherland's Project Sketchpad. As users drew on Sketchpad's display with the attached light pen, they reinforced associative connections between activity and perception: Make this movement and that line will appear on screen. In all the years since, that basic relationship has been articulated in uncountable ways, but has never been improved upon. The essence of Sketchpad lies in the relation between hand and eye: Body, perception, and cognition.

Just before Sutherland created Sketchpad, J. C. R Licklider framed man–computer symbiosis as a powerful aid to cognition. And despite being a psychologist, Licklider had not imagined that symbiosis could manipulate the human mind. Nor had Sutherland – at the start. But in the three years between Sketchpad and his "Ultimate Display" white paper, Sutherland began to see how computing could be used to shape the perceptions and, thereby, the minds of its users – invoking *Alice's Adventures in Wonderland* as his example.

Sutherland's experiments in perception and cognition fundamentally shaped the direction of computing. Within a decade, the concept of a computer screen as a playground for visual metaphors saw the birth of modern computer interfaces. At Xerox's Palo Alto Research Center (PARC), users typed into "windows" that could be manipulated – that is, dragged around by a mouse – as if physically present. Those same windows could be "scrolled" – like unrolling a window shade – to reveal hidden content. On-screen "buttons" could be "pressed" via the mouse, to initiate actions and trigger the execution of computer programs.[4]

Half a century later, all of this feels impossibly remedial: That's how computers work. While the elements of the graphical user interface (GUI) might seem more artistic than representational, every on-screen element and activity had to withstand endless user testing and review before it made its way into the toolkit of these first-generation interfaces. That user testing focused on the cognitive load involved in exploring, intuiting, and mastering each of these elements. Could someone with no prior experience with a GUI have a meaningfully productive relationship with it? Would the user know what to do? Would they need a human guide? A manual? Or would they just be able to work it all out from the visual metaphors and their responses to user actions delivered by both keyboard and mouse? Would it just work?

In the early 1970s, researchers knew very little about what comprised an effective interface element, so they tried many different experiments, the overwhelming majority of which failed. The few that succeeded – still in widespread use today – have faded into invisibility. Users now see through the interface to the task at hand.

All of this fundamental research work entered public consciousness on January 24, 1984, when Steve Jobs unveiled Apple Computer's Macintosh. Embodying all of the lessons learned at Xerox PARC (Jobs had visited the facility a few years earlier, leaving with a new vision for computing, and for Apple), Macintosh turned computing as metaphor into a mass-market product.

To compete against the then-dominant IBM PC, Apple's Macintosh needed a broad range of software applications, and for that, the firm would need to educate its developer community on the details of a very different kind of human–computer interface. All of this information reached developers in two publications: The three-volume *Inside Macintosh* – covering the details of Macintosh interface programming; and – more significantly – Apple's book *Human Interface Guidelines*. *Human Interface Guidelines* summarized everything both Xerox PARC and Apple had learned about how to construct GUIs that guided the user into doing the right thing every time, avoiding design confusion and cognitive overload – such as asking the user to remember too much about the state and operation of the computer. Follow these guidelines, Apple instructed, and the user will always know how to use your program, never getting lost or growing frustrated.

Within a decade, nearly every computer used visual metaphors, managed by physical interaction, controlled via a mouse. Sutherland's vision for computing had become synonymous with computing. It had all worked – though not for Apple. Software monopolist Microsoft created its own GUI-based operating system, Windows, using its partnerships with IBM, Intel, and the growing PC-compatible marketplace to get Windows onto every PC sold.

At this point personal computers mostly occupied a niche as business machines – good for word processing and numerical modeling with a spreadsheet, but little else. The GUI revolution made those features easy to access with a minimum of training, thereby leading to the sudden mass obsolescence of a whole class of secretarial labor. But the average person still had little reason to use a computer in their daily lives.

Tim Berners-Lee's "World Wide Web" began in 1989 as a project to link the heterogeneous computer systems used at European atom-smasher CERN,[5] and over five years grew into a broader solution, capable of connecting all of the data on all of the computers everywhere on Earth into a single, interlinked whole. In the process, the World Wide Web redefined computing – by slapping a GUI across *all* human knowledge. Via the Web, computing and knowledge became inseparable.

While the Web provided immediate benefits to business computer users (for example, documentation and manuals could be published online, available to all, and updated instantly), its true value came from the fervor it inspired in all of the millions of users who came to it with more quotidian needs: Who has a good recipe for blueberry pie? Is this skin condition dangerous? What kind of flower is this? These more modest requests – and their replies, either found on a website, or in responses from other Web users – created the real value of the Web: It respected and responded to our needs.[6]

The Web could only do this because it rested upon decades of research work on GUIs. From its earliest days, the Web continuously evolved its interfaces toward clearer and more apprehensible metaphors. Kevin Hughes, a researcher working at the University of Hawai'i, wrapped an image of a button around a clickable Web element, creating the first "button" on the Web – the prototype for hundreds of thousands of interface innovations.[7]

Much of the early Web now looks eye-wateringly ugly – clumsy and unsophisticated. But just as Xerox PARC and Apple had conducted their own experiments on possible interfaces, so the thousands of designers and engineers of the Web engaged in their own interface experiments – elements so common today we no longer see them, such as menus, tabs, and zoomable images.

The workflow of the Web encourages experimentation: Designers propose new elements to engineers who then build them. Those features can be released immediately, and immediately tested on users. Because of the nature of the Web as an inherently connected, always-on medium, the results of these experiments can be known immediately. Rather than having a dedicated

Via the Web, computing and knowledge became inseparable.

testing facility, such as that run by Apple, a Web firm simply publishes its latest interface to a public and popular page, then observes as the results pour in.

These tests often measure the results of a tried-and-true design element against a new one. Such "A/B tests" have become a staple of Web design, particularly in firms that fetishize data-driven decision making, such as Google. Over its first decade, the Web became a universal interface to human knowledge – as well as a universal test bed for the metaphors used to access and manipulate that knowledge.

This tight coupling between experiment, testing, analysis, and adjustment – leading to a new round of experiments, testing, analysis, and adjustments – meant that the Web rapidly matured as an interface to information. At the same time – though invisibly – it matured as an analytic medium. Psychologists wrote tests, mathematicians built statistical analysis models, and data scientists fed huge amounts of user testing data into tools whose outputs began to drive not just the look of a website, but the decisions of the business behind it. Businesses had to master the subtle relationship between customers and data, or they would risk being driven out of the market by businesses that did. AltaVista, the Web's first practical search engine, lost out to Google because it never learned how to feed its own user activities back into its design. Other Web businesses sought to avoid making a similar unforced error, focusing on learning everything they could from their user data to make their sites ever easier – and "stickier."

"Stickiness" entered the vocabulary of Web design shortly after the collapse of the massive tech bubble at the start of the twenty-first century. Like a metaphorical fly paper, it points toward an interface and experience so engaging and fulfilling that users linger longer. Shoppers would buy more. Subscribers would read more. Listeners would hear more. Since many Web-based publishers funded their operations through advertising, stickiness presented a path to greater revenues – using data-driven design to increase the time a user spent visiting a site.

Websites needed to measure their stickiness through a continuous observation of users, inserting code into web pages that accurately tracked how long a user spent on a page, where they stopped, where they passed over quickly, and where they left the site. Initially, this helped designers develop websites that increased the overall engagement of their users. It worked: Using these data-driven measurements and improvements, users spent more time – and money – on sticky sites.

Simultaneously, users became the focus of targeted Web advertising. Google used data gleaned from user searches to provide contextually relevant ads to that user: Someone searching for travel to Paris might see ads for hotels in Paris, or rental cars, or cheap flights, and so forth. In order to provide these ads across a range of different websites – almost all of which used Google's advertising platform – the search engine firm began to build profiles of its millions of users. As they swelled with data, these profiles became increasingly useful. Gathered through observation, historical data found value as a predictive tool. Capturing both the long-term interests and fleeting passions of an individual, profiles revealed more about those individuals than they would ever willingly reveal, a depth of insight that increased the effectiveness of targeted advertising, as that profile became a sort of digital alter ego, encompassing all that could be known about a person via their online interactions.[8]

The smartphone sent this superheated environment of stickiness into overdrive, inheriting everything Apple had learned across more than 30 years of experiments in interface design – together with everything Google had learned about tracking and profiling the Web's users. As a handheld and utterly personal device, the smartphone became the focus for a new generation of interface development *and* at the same time the enabling technology for a quantum leap in user profiling.

Users carried their smartphones everywhere because Apple had embedded their best, most refined interaction design lessons into iPhone, so the device gave pleasure to its users. This meant the smartphone saw far more consistent use than any other device in the history of computing; not just in the office, but on the street, in the home – even in bed. Within a few years, half of all smartphone owners slept next to their devices every night.[9]

That continuous, close relationship between a smartphone and its owner meant the tracking and profiling data suddenly became far more detailed, specific, and real time. No longer confined to the stretches in front of a desktop-bound Web browser, smartphone users sent search data to Google throughout their daily activities, often accompanied by location data that situated those searches in time and space. The user profile grew far beyond its beginnings as a list of likes and interests, into something that began to resemble a simulacrum of the smartphone user – a *Doppelgänger* and digital twin.

Google now understood how its users lived their lives – day-to-day, moment-to-moment; saw the routes they took to work, where they shopped for dinner, and how many hours they spent at home, asleep. All of that data made it possible to predict and anticipate user needs – both from historical analysis of that user's behavior, and via a comparative analysis across the behavior of millions of other similar users.

The contextually relevant ads Google sent to its profiled users via the customers of its advertising platforms quickly gathered the lion's share of the marketplace for digital advertising, commanding the highest fees precisely because the ad would be seen by a user predisposed to be interested in it. The great gap between advertiser and audience, bridged by the concatenation of smartphone and profiling, made Google one of the most valuable companies in the world.

Where Google had to observe its users in order to profile them, sites such as Friendster, MySpace, Twitter, and "The Facebook" offered themselves up as social publication platforms where people freely shared their activities, reflections, and connections, both with the other users of these websites, and – though less noticeably – with the owners of those sites.

In 2004, when The Facebook only reached students enrolled at Harvard University, Mark Zuckerberg exchanged messages with a friend, a conversation that came to light when reported by *Business Insider* in 2018:[10]

Zuckerberg: Yeah so if you ever need info about anyone at Harvard.

Zuckerberg: Just ask.
Zuckerberg: I have over 4,000 emails, pictures, addresses, SNS.
[Friend]: What? How'd you manage that one?
Zuckerberg: People just submitted it.
Zuckerberg: I don't know why.
Zuckerberg: They "trust me."
Zuckerberg: Dumb fucks.

The desire to share, to connect, to know and be known – together with the range of narcissistic impulses we all fall prey to – all contributed to the explosive growth of social media over the first decade of the century.

Although the content shared revealed quite a bit about these sites' users, its enduring value lay in the "social graph" – the network of connections and affiliations. Researchers soon realized that a social graph revealed more about a site's user than any information provided by the user – or any data that could be gathered from a user profile. Political leanings, sexual preference, marital status, physical characteristics, and much, much more could be abstracted from a social graph analysis.[11]

Zuckerberg's Facebook won the social media contest, growing past a billion monthly users shortly after its May 2012 public share offering. Answerable now to its shareholders – who had been told to expect continued, meteoric growth in both users and revenues – Facebook confronted its first growth crisis, as users, drowned by a tsunami of sharing, pulled back from the platform.

The solution to Facebook's problems came via Facebook chief operating officer (COO) Sheryl Sandberg.

Sandberg had successfully grown Google's ad business, learning the value of the deep profiling of users, amplified by Google's relentlessly data-driven approach to testing and refinement. All of this became core strategy for Facebook, as it incorporated continuous user profiling into its activities.[12] A user now had two profiles: The public profile they generated as a result of their sharing activities; and an invisible, digital twin profile created by their interactions.

In an act with far-reaching consequences, Facebook now used that digital twin as a way to curate a user's public profile. Rather than an unfiltered feed of all the activities of all of a user's connections, the digital twin would be used as a guide for how to filter that feed, prioritizing those feed elements that produced the greatest stickiness. Facebook watched its users exploring their feeds, learned which elements produced the greatest engagement, and used this to edit the feed to emphasize similarly engaging elements.[13] These changes drove Facebook's user engagement to new heights, pleased shareholders, and cemented Sandberg's reputation as a key contributor to Facebook's success.

The specifics of engagement vary from individual to individual, but underneath all of it, engagement measures emotion. We find it difficult to resist topics that please us – or enrage us. At both ends of the emotional spectrum, we "stick." At the same time, it became clear that the emotional state of a Facebook user could be accurately gauged by that user's inter-action with emotional content. Angry or sad users tended to gravitate toward elements reinforcing those feelings, while happy users tended toward upbeat elements. As all of this poured into the invisible digital twin maintained by Facebook, the firm realized it had created a real-time barometer revealing an individual's emotional state. Moreover, a 2014 research project (conducted without securing appropriate permissions from test subjects) showed that Facebook could manipulate its users' emotions by varying the feed elements: Add more negativity, and an individual's emotional state would decline toward sadness; more positivity and the individual would be happier.[14]

Through its profiling, Facebook developed an emotional monitor of its users *and* a tool for emotional manipulation, an incredible concatenation of powers they immediately set to work to monetize. This came to light in a 2017 slide deck created by the leadership of its Australian division, a story that exploded onto the front page of the May 1, 2017 issue of the national broadsheet, *The Australian*:

> Facebook is using sophisticated algorithms to identify and exploit Australians as young as 14, by allowing advertisers to target them at their most vulnerable, including when they feel "worthless" and "insecure," secret internal documents reveal ... Facebook is not only able to detect sentiment, but it can also understand how emotions are communicated.[15]

The article exposed the confidential inner workings of a social network that knew far more about the real-time emotional states of its users – particularly its under-age users – than had ever been revealed, and showed that Facebook shopped this real-time capability to undermine the emotional security and well-being of its users to its advertising partners.

Caught red-handed, Facebook quickly issued an apology and began an internal investigation – but they'd already tipped their hand, showing the incredible insight they had into their users' emotional state, and the enormous power that conferred. Feeding observations of user behavior into a "hidden" profile, then using that to shape the emotional engagement of the elements in a user's feed created a relationship grounded in manipulation: Gaslighting by algorithm.

Consistently downplaying its role as a mass manipulator, Facebook managed to avoid any serious scrutiny of its practices, even after this exposure of the manipulation of emotionally vulnerable teenagers. Then the social media giant's relationship to political profiling and targeting firm Cambridge Analytica came to light. Suddenly, Facebook seemed to threaten the underpinnings of democratic processes throughout the world: Brexit, Trump, and Kenya's 2017 election all appear to have been interfered with via Cambridge Analytica's careful profiling and targeting of Facebook users.[16]

Politicians and the public took notice, forcing Facebook into a response: It promised to adjust the feed to be more representative and less engaging. But that caught the firm on the horns of a dilemma: Its enormous success as an advertising platform (generator of the lion's share of the firm's revenues) relied upon its high levels of engagement. Change the algorithm to decrease engagement and a corresponding drop in revenues could result. Facebook had become so addicted to the algorithmic manipulations that made the site so addictive to users that neither Facebook nor Facebook's users seemed able to change their behaviors, and break the cycle.

The seemingly inescapable and ever-tightening feedback loop between Facebook and its users demonstrates a singular point about network technologies deployed at scale: Such systems can produce effects that cannot easily be managed. The sheer joy of Sutherland's Sketchpad or Apple's iPhone means one thing when the loop encompasses only the user and their device, and something else entirely when that loop expands to include other users and other networked actors.

Networked systems express capacities and tendencies that emerge over time, neither designed with intent nor foreseen by their creators. The progression in Facebook's efforts from increasing user engagement to Cambridge Analytica's electoral manipulations seems, in retrospect, quite predictable – a straight line drawn from Norbert Wiener's observations made nearly 70 years earlier in *The Human Use of Human Beings*. Despite Wiener's warnings, none of it had been anticipated. Nor, once such a system had emerged, could it easily be dismantled – but it could easily be copied. Facebook created a twenty-first-century blueprint for surveillance, profiling, and manipulation available to any organization – commercial, governmental, or subversive – seeking to manipulate the public. Through a set of finely observed and highly tuned techniques Facebook targeted individuals at scale, and thereby achieved mass influence.

The whole technological project inherits this new capability. Every device with connectivity and capacity

Networked systems express capacities and tendencies that emerge over time, neither designed with intent nor foreseen by their creators.

to observe its environment carries within it the seed of this sort of capacity. It only requires an intent to activate by the designer. Emotional profiling and manipulation have become additional elements in the toolkit of interface. This is Facebook's gift.

This is not wholly Facebook's doing, even if their own efforts brought this process to an unwholesome culmination. Every development to deepen human–computer interaction (even from before Sutherland) led to the development of systems so potent they can now overwhelm us psychically – just as a steam engine has long been able to overpower us physically.

The consequences of that sudden shift in the power balance between ourselves and our devices have become today's commonplaces: Smartphones that people seem unable to put down, or look away from, or leave unattended for more than a few moments.[17] Even when their own lives, or the lives of their loved ones, hang in the balance.

That reordering of priorities points toward the "addictive" qualities of these interactive media, and points back to a path, more than half a century long, that led from the first triumphs in human–computer interaction to a world where those interactions have thoroughly colonized our consciousness, depriving us of agency. Research, experiment, and endless testing led us here. Now that we can experiment and test at planetary scale, and feed the results of those tests into cloud-based artificial intelligence programs, this kind of addictive engagement can be consumed as ubiquitously as electricity or running water.

Although none of this happened overnight, it feels new

to us, and that lack of perspective has its twin in a lack of insight. We do not recognize that these machines have consistently grown more engaging, so we did not see the moment when that engagement overwhelmed our native and naïve capacities to resist. Instead of seeing the device for what it is – an addiction with digital characteristics – we look for a way out: A release via another device.

In April 2012, Google's X division – in charge of all their "moonshot" research projects – announced their first attempt at an augmented reality display, Google Glass.[18] Lacking SLAM capabilities, Glass served more as a display device for an attached smartphone than as an "ultimate display." Glass could only broadly orient itself in space, providing a heads-up overlay of textual information presented in one corner of the user's field-of-view. This information could be contextually relevant – information about that location – or notifications from a messaging app, and so on. With its built-in camera, Glass could also record and even stream video from the user over the network.

Google co-founder Sergey Brin became the public champion for Glass. In early 2013 he gave a talk at the tech-heavy TED Conference, in which he proclaimed Glass as the solution for our smartphone addictions, as reported in the *Guardian*:

> [The smartphone is] kind of emasculating. Is this what you're meant to do with your body? Is this the way you're meant to interact with other people? Is the future of connection just people walking around hunched up, looking down, rubbing a featureless piece of glass? ... You want something that will free your eyes.[19]

Although *The Guardian* – and the broader public – focused on (and lampooned) the use of the word "emasculating," Brin's curious phrasing pointed toward something that had, to that point, only rarely been noted: The ever-increasing lure of the smartphone screen. Brin, perhaps, finds ideas of agency and masculinity closely congruent, and anything that deprives people of agency would, in that sense, be framed as emasculating. Conversely, according to Brin, Google's Glass restored balance in human–computer interactions by bringing our gaze up, away from the device, out onto the world. Brin pitched Glass to TED attendees as the solution for the problems created by another Google product – its Android smartphone operating system, which had already claimed nearly 90 percent of the global market. *Here's a technical solution*, Brin seems to be saying, *to the technical problem that we created.*

But a solution with problems.

In the years following the introduction and market failure of Google Glass, smartphones grew more alluring. The inputs of billions of users, carefully recorded and profiled, then fed back to them in edited form, tempted them with engagements that had been analytically demonstrated to be progressively more difficult to resist.

In the second half of the 2010s, the human race disappeared behind screens. Parents gave small children screens to soothe and occupy them. These same parents tapped anxiously at their own screens, looking for moments of connection, reassurance, or escape. Grandparents checked their own feeds for news from other grandparents about their grandchildren – who mostly eschewed Facebook for newer apps, like Snap and TikTok. The idea of "disconnection" – away from screens, and from the nearly pervasive coverage of mobile broadband signals – became anathema, associated with being stranded or lost, and unable to summon aid. In less than a generation, the cultural norms of connection, communication, and community inverted into a condition identified by psychologist Sherry Turkle as being "alone together,"[20] a desperate stroking of inanimate objects in search of human contact.

Within this supersaturated environment of observation, engagement, and addiction, when fully-featured AR mirrorshades come to market, sometime in the mid-2020s, they will be hailed as the complete solution to the problem of the smartphone. These new devices will offer a freedom from the screen that Brin's Google Glass promised, but could not deliver – too early, too minimal, and too confronting. Another decade of development will see the prototypical designs of both Glass and HoloLens resolve into something light, attractive, potent – and undeniably engaging. Believing that they'll recover their agency from the hegemony of the smartphone screen, millions of users will buy these spectacles, achieving the desired release as they look up and out, rather than down into the device. But at what cost?

Even when held directly before the eyes, a smartphone screen occupies only a tiny portion of a user's field of view. Users make a decision to give the device their attention. (Though it must be acknowledged that some of the agency in that decision has been spirited away by techniques of engagement.) Behind augmented reality mirrorshades, the screen becomes the entire world.

There is no place that is not screen. This means that a user never needs to gaze at a screen – because, entirely enveloped by it, they cannot look away. The price of liberation from the smartphone screen? Imprisonment within another, total, screen.

For many – perhaps most – this will be seen as a fair bargain. They will adopt AR mirrorshades because they represent the recovery of a quality of experience that nearly disappeared in the 2010s – a screen-free existence. Even though AR mirrorshades represent the final triumph of the screen as the "ultimate display," because that screen has disappeared, it will not be seen for what it is – everything. This foreground/background reversal of display and environment represents the key identifying characteristic of augmented reality: In virtual reality the screen is the world; in augmented reality, *there is no screen other than the world.*

These invisible yet ubiquitous screens inherit all of the qualities and characteristics of all earlier technologies of networked interactivity. Far less a new beginning than an extension and continuation of the existing and ever-deepening techniques of observation, analysis, and feedback, AR mirrorshades offer an unprecedented opportunity to scrutinize user interactions in minute detail. Their cameras, depth sensors, GPS, and accelerometers that enable SLAM within an AR display locate the user in space, but, far more than this, they also provide information about gaze direction; that is, where the user's eyes look. This granular information about the sensory interests of users has never before been possible – except in laboratory environments where eyeball position can be read via the reflection of infrared light. Gaze direction sensing comes as basic function-ality in AR displays: In order to work at all, these displays must know what the user's gaze encompasses.[21]

Although necessary for the proper operation of an AR display, user gaze data has a far more valuable quality – as a highly accurate measure of engagement. People look at things that they find engaging; and this engagement largely bypasses any cultural filters. We often look at something because of our compulsions. User gaze data opens a doorway into a subtle aspect of human nature, one that, though acknowledged, has been difficult to observe – except in the laboratory. Gaze direction speaks volumes about what really interests us, compels us, frightens us, or excites us. It speaks directly to those parts of us barely mediated by culture and convention. That makes it rare, valuable – and incredibly potent.

Turning the world into the screen effectively turns it into a browsable environment. In much the same way that a finger "mouses" its way across a smartphone screen, gaze direction provides notification of intention and interest. Where that information remains entirely within the device, it can be used to resolve detail (for example, staring at something can reveal additional detail about it) or otherwise improve the browsing experience.[22] However, all of the currently available or planned AR displays have been designed to operate as networked display devices. It seems unlikely that gaze direction would remain local to the device – any more than selections and finger gestures made within a smart-phone app today remain within the smartphone.

Smartphone apps profile users through their interac-tions, streaming that interaction data back to the cloud via the network, where it can be profiled, analyzed, and fed back to the user as increasing engagement. Networked AR devices will likely stream user gaze data into the cloud, where it can be dissected to learn everything possible about the user's engagement within the environment presented by the device. How long did a user gaze at that hologram? Or that billboard? Did they miss a step, stop short, or keep walking along?

All of that data – and much, much more – will be exposed in an analysis of gaze data. When added together with all of the other sensors – GPS, accelerometers, depth cameras, microphones, and so on – networked AR displays reveal themselves as the most valuable apparatus for the direct measurement of user interaction since the dawn of the field. Surveillance plus network analysis means rapid user profiling of enormous depth.

From the moment a user dons their "ultimate display," they feed data into the device's sensors, which sift through that torrent of sensor data, distilling it into a manageable, meaningful stream that can be uploaded into the cloud. At that point what happens depends largely on the good graces of the firm providing the network connection. Firms like Google, Apple, and Facebook will offer complete solutions, owning and controlling every part of the system, from head-mounted hardware through to apps to the cloud-based systems used to process and analyze user interactions.

While Apple has shown little interest in the analysis of user interactions – trumpeting privacy as its key point of competitive difference – both Google and Facebook built trillion-dollar businesses upon their ability to profile and target users. Both can be expected to do everything in their power to monetize gaze data.

Google will want to note how long users gaze at all of the ads placed into and upon their synthetic environments, and, beyond that, will use gaze data as an additional service to clients who offer outdoor advertising (signs and billboards) in addition to digital offerings. Gaze data adds value to advertising, and makes Google's ad services more valuable to advertisers. Google's motivations around user gaze data seem straightforward.

Facebook – given both its history and predilections – presents a more concerning use case: Increasing user engagement through subtle, continuous modifications in the synthetic elements of the world. As the social media giant currently uses this technique to increase user engagement on its website and apps, and can algorithmically tune that engagement with great precision, rather like turning a dial, they will have the capacity to apply the same general techniques to their own AR displays.

Although a relative newcomer to virtual and augmented reality, in 2014 Mark Zuckerberg made up for his tardiness with the three-billion-dollar purchase of VR startup Oculus.[23] Under Facebook, Oculus has developed a modestly successful line of both smartphone-based and stand-alone virtual reality products. None of this contributes meaningfully to Facebook's bottom line (it's likely a cost center rather than a profit engine), but it has helped to align the firm with the potential of a post-smartphone world of AR displays.

In his 2017 keynote at Facebook's F8 developer conference, after acknowledging the degree of difficulty associated with bringing AR mirrorshades to market, Zuckerberg spent 20 minutes demonstrating the extensive AR capabilities in the latest version of its smartphone app. With its immense installed base, Facebook has likely brought AR to more users than any other firm – within an app known to continuously profile user interactions.

That profiling already extends into Facebook's VR products. As *PC Magazine* reported in December 2019, Facebook had begun informing users of its Oculus VR headsets that their behaviors would be monitored and profiled while using its products:

> Oculus VR headset owners be aware: Your Oculus activity can now be used to serve up customized ads on your connected Facebook account ... "As part of these changes, Facebook will now use information about your Oculus activity ... to help provide these new social features and more relevant content, including ads," it said.[24]

When it comes to market, a Facebook AR display can continuously profile its users, using the full array of sensory inputs, including gaze detection, developing a precisely detailed map of their engagements. When paired with a Facebook-delivered environment that mixes the real world with synthetic additions, Facebook would then know both the user's reactions to the real-world environment and any changes produced by those synthetic additions – information that could then be used to modify those additions to make them more engaging, or, conversely, to make a real-world location less engaging.

Facebook already has the capacity – demonstrated within its smartphone app – to generate a reality so engaging that users find it difficult to look away from it. The same will be true for the users of its AR products. Those users will be inserted into another reality, one of Facebook's making, based on their carefully analyzed profile data. As with our smartphones, as AR becomes more engaging, it becomes more difficult to leave behind, becoming the default source of reality.

This power to create emotional engagement (either attachment or revulsion) with a synthetic reality will simply be the re-embodiment of Facebook's current business model. Nothing will be private to the user; instead, all data valuable for the development of a user profile will be gathered, in order to provide the most effective insight into that user's emotional state, locating the most potent levers for managing that state. As this is how the firm already treats its users – a resource that can be observed and emotionally monetized – it's difficult to imagine a world where Facebook would or even could behave differently.

AR devices need to read us in order to create their illusions. We become an open book. Once they read us, they use what they've read to write upon us. Who gets to read those books?

Disconnected from the network, an AR system can do little beyond creating a few spectacular effects. These systems need network connections in order to achieve any utility. Without that connection they're nearly pointless toys; with that connection they become almost impossibly potent – and potentially dangerous.

Fortunately, connectivity need not be measured in binary all-or-nothing terms. Between pulling the plug and blowing the dam lies a rich region of possibility – and agency. How much does a device need to share? Can that sharing be kept to a bare minimum for a given task? Can a user be made aware of the data being collected, uploaded, profiled, then fed back to them as modifications to engagement? How can an AR display be designed to offer maximum transparency, both in its operation, and in the actions of all of the parties to its operation? Can we uncouple a device from the cloud it connects itself to, offering users a choice of providers of synthetic modifications to the world?

The devices of the 2010s – Glass and HoloLens, both primitive compared to what will follow on from them in the 2020s – answer none of these questions, offering no practical agency to their users. The device comes as a piece, a sort of technological "body without organs," meant to be apprehended as a whole; not just in its physical components but in all of its networked capacities, agencies, and agendas. Such devices present a smooth surface of stage magic, in order to preserve an illusion of transparency – that this device is simply what it seems to be, and not an interface for sensing, profiling, and feeding user interactions back as emotional engagements.

All AR systems, from any manufacturer, raise these same questions. Facebook may be among the most notorious bad actors in technology, but they operate within, and take their lead from, a longer tradition of

As AR becomes more engaging, it becomes more difficult to leave behind, becoming the default source of reality.

permissiveness that inevitably sacrifices user agency to serve the ends of a business. Because they sit so close to us, interactive technologies can excite or antagonize us. As they get closer to our skin – and augmented reality brings them very close – their capacity for producing emotional responses grows exponentially.[25]

Questions around the ends of interactivity – asking what a human might be capable of with a capable interface to computing – inspired much of the original work in the field. As this work achieves many of the ends foreseen by Sutherland in his "Ultimate Display" white paper, these questions become paramount – of greater importance than any of the many technical difficulties that remain within the field. Now that we can do this, why we do it is more important than how.

We can already construct AR displays capable of profiling user interaction so precisely that they can be used to drive emotional engagement to levels never before possible with any other medium. In the few years before we begin manufacturing such devices by the billions, we must name and frame these new potentials in a way that allows us to be able to resist their allure. Otherwise, we can confidently predict that, just as we were once unable to look away from smartphone screens, we will find ourselves unable to remove our AR mirrorshades, enthralled by another reality, while losing the tether to our own. Hidden behind those mirrorshades, people could quickly become unable to face an unfiltered reality, one lacking smooth, invisible emotional adjustments and engagements.

Should that happen, the "emasculations" of Sergey Brin's smartphone users will have returned with an unimagined potency. In 2013, Brin suggested a techno-logical solution to a technological problem – but one that exponentially amplifies the underlying problem. In the 2020s, AR mirrorshades will be offered as the "antidote" to the smartphone, just as heroin was once offered up as a cure to morphine addiction.

Yet, despite all of these obvious dangers – and the dangers we cannot yet see but which will undoubtedly come as AR devices achieve global scale – a strong case can be made for the widespread adoption of augmented reality as a necessary tool for operating within a world that has become not only less transparent in its activities, but, in many important aspects, has disappeared from view completely. It's in this capacity – as revelator – that AR will touch an essential – and pre existing – need. Satisfying this need will make AR indispensably useful.

4

The Web Wide World

Today's cinema audiences have access to enormous libraries of screen content – television, film, and video games. Since the late 2000s, games have earned more than film box office (though films regularly offer ancillary revenues that video games only rarely exploit), so audiences come to the cinema with an awareness of all of the conventions of screen entertainment, plus many hours of interactions with highly responsive inter-active entertainment experiences.

In his 2020 film for Disney Studios, *Free Guy*, Ryan Reynolds – Hollywood's highest-profile satirist – set fire to many of the tropes of those games. Named after the ubiquitous, unremarkable, and disposable non-playing characters (NPCs) that have populated video games since their beginnings, *Free Guy* imagines what might happen if an NPC – played by Reynolds – suddenly gained agency; capable of doing, rather than just being done to.

Throwing the logic of the film's game universe into chaos (it borrows freely from such genre-defining titles as *Grand Theft Auto* and *Fallout*, where players can explore and interact with the game world at their leisure), Reynold's NPC seizes a weapon from a bank robber, uses it to kill them, then realizes he's still holding onto the robber's sunglasses. When "Free Guy" steps outside that bank, he dons the sunglasses – and the entire film pivots.

Suddenly, the world reveals itself: The words "Bank Heist" appear in the middle of the air – a nod to the "mission" genre of video games. Overlaid with information, the environment exposes its inner, hidden qualities. The most ordinary things now betray their significance – and Free Guy, overwhelmed, takes the sunglasses off. Everything returns to normal. Sunglasses back on – and the world is again revealed – Free Guy responds with the word of wonder, "Wow," then begins to explore his newly revealed world.

Nothing about this feels unusual to a video game player. From the earliest days of text-based adventure games, players have been able to inspect game worlds and their contents, in search of clues, cues, and other characters. Digital games have always been endowed with a quality of interiority because of their essential nature as constructions of information. Information describes an object within a game world – for the needs of the logic of that world. That information allows the game to operate logically.

Equivalently, information can be used to describe an object for the benefit of the players of the game.[1] This information means nothing (or very little) to the game itself. Yet that digital flotsam – known as "metadata," as it sits above and outside of functional information representations – can have immense meaning to the players, who may find themselves engaged by, drawn to, or repelled from certain courses of action based on what they learn from that metadata. Game logic and the "rules" of the game (metadata as perceived by human players) can collude, or collide; neither quite depends upon the other. Where they work together, the game helps its players along toward their goals. When at variance, they force the player to explore and learn to exploit the systems designed to resist them. Both offer opportunities for play, as we explore and learn how to manage our engagement around a game, its environment, and metadata.

Until the moment he donned AR mirrorshades, Reynold's Free Guy remained constrained by the rules of the game. Previously an innocent in this world, his AR mirrorshades give him information and context. Informed by the game's metadata, Free Guy has the information he needs to make decisions in his own best interest. A non-playing character becomes a game player, locating and consuming in-game resources meant for players, such as the red suitcase with a white cross floating above the ground that slowly spins. Game players would immediately recognize this as a "health" pack, capable of helping a player recover from injuries. Reaching for the pack, Free Guy gets a charge of health that makes him feel giddy and high, and Reynold's character now knows those AR mirrorshades offer more than meaning – they can mean the difference between life and death. Why would Free Guy ever take them off?

Creating information about our world – metadata – has always been an essential element of human culture. We live within a world – once largely natural, lately increasingly artificial – so rich in diversity, danger, and opportunity that to pass through it without the guidance and insight of those who have passed this way before would leave us at a perpetual disadvantage. We'd be forever putting ourselves in peril as we explored an unknown world, rather than following the careful paths laid down before us.

Social species like humans use their sociability to share information about their environment: What are the hazards? Predators? Prey? Safety and shelter? Answers to all of these vital questions can be held within the mind and memory of a group, affixed to the external landscape through experience or via instruction. This leaf; this cave; this shoreline – each has its stories, gathered by experience, distilled through memory, and transformed into knowledge. Each generation mentors the next, enhancing opportunities and warning against dangers.

With the development of writing, space could be inscribed with warning signs or instructions. The origins of metadata go back at least 6,000 years, all the way to Sumer and Egypt – but arguably begin well before that: 50,000-year-old petroglyphs found in the Kimberley region of Australia clearly illustrate local fauna.[2] For as long as humans have drawn, we've inscribed stories about the experience of place – metadata.

Maps represent a common form of metadata; sharing what is known about place, along with a representation of that place, itself a form of metadata. As the world grew more populated and civilized, maps became more detailed and more stylized, metadata shaping representation, so that, as in a well-designed subway map, the representation itself becomes another type of metadata.

By the early 1990s, much of the human world had been well described by metadata. With the exception of inscriptions and signs, this wealth of information lay at some distance from the environments it described. The map is not the territory; ignorance cast a shadow in the space between them. Having information about nearly anything anyone might experience, anywhere, did not mean having it at hand. There might be metadata, even vitally important metadata, but where?

That question would be answered by the World Wide Web. The Web linked diverse information resources into a cohesive whole, regardless of location, organization, affiliation, or technology. Ultimately agnostic, the Web quickly became a level playing field for all informational resources. The Web accepted all, refusing none – content and meaning, together with metadata (content about content and meaning about meaning) – creating an undifferentiated sea of information, universally accessible at every point. It soon became an unknowable and unnavigable mess.

This led to the creation of "index" metadata – information about Web content – powering the earliest version of Yahoo!, and providing a consistent, ordered, catalog-like interface to the wealth of information published to the Web.[3] That indexing proved so successful – and made the Web so useful for so many people, who had never before had access to the metadata they needed at the time and place that they needed it – that it created the conditions for an explosive increase in both the use of the Web and the number of Web publishers. A catalog such as Yahoo! can be managed by people if it grows linearly; where it grows exponentially (as it did, during the last five years of the twentieth century), it overwhelms all category, drowning order in a riot of growth.

Although essential in 1995, within just a handful of years Yahoo! no longer offered the kind of support Web users needed to find relevant metadata. Instead, Web users turned to search engine AltaVista. Rather than adopting a human-curated system of categorization, AltaVista "crawled" the entirety of the Web, continuously scanning for new sites, new pages, and changed content, adding all of that information to its own database, in order to create its own metadata. Users of AltaVista could type text into a search box, and a list of content closely matching the search term would be returned, leaving the user to make their own decisions about the relevance of any of those responses. AltaVista worked well enough to power the Web past the bottleneck of human-curated categories, opening the era of the "machine Web" – information indexed and ordered by algorithms.[4]

When two Stanford graduate students realized that the Web provided its own, contextually relevant, metadata through its hyperlinks,[5] recognizing that content linked to other content serves as a fair proxy for relevance, they built a search engine – Google – that quickly outclassed AltaVista in its capacity to direct users to the information they sought. These cascading improvements in search increased the utility of the Web, again attracting more users and creating an endless demand for more content, a feedback loop of use leading to creation leading to use leading to creation. Less than a decade after Yahoo! launched, Google indexed a Web measured in the billions of pages, with hundreds of millions of daily users.

Very little of the Web content indexed by Google contained any explicit metadata; instead, computers would read the content, parse it for meaning with ever-increasing accuracy, and use that derived meaning as a form of metadata. This meant that although the Web could be searched quickly and efficiently, it bore only a weak relationship to the world beyond. The Web pointed to itself, and only to itself. At the end of its first decade, the Web articulated the human universe in a spaceless dimension of information that had no enduring connections to place.

Yet by this point an enormous amount of information about space had already been created and published to the Web: Maps, building plans, indices, addresses, layouts, physical and mechanical blueprints – all of it information connected to specific places, digitized and accessible. Lacking metadata – effectively spaceless – this content lacked context, and, denied context, lost most of its utility. A detailed map of a building that has no connection to the building itself provides too much information and too little order.

Some of this disconnection can be attributed to the devices used to create and consume Web content. Computers in the 1990s and early 2000s could not operate comfortably from the palm of one's hand. A computer – even a portable computer – weighed multiple kilograms and stayed put when in use. Apple's iPhone introduced the idea of fully featured smartphone computing – locatively aware via GPS and other sensors in a way that had never been seriously considered by the designers of desktop-class machines.

Culminating that process of cascading improvements, the smartphone brought the Web to everyone, everywhere, all the time. It became possible (and reasonable) to search for, find, and use relevant information at the moment of need. This ability to access all of human knowledge instantly, easily, and in context – and not the ability to make calls, send messages, or play music – proved the real hook for smartphone users. A smartphone plus Google put a searchable interface to all human knowledge into the palm of a user's hand. Although not always put to work, it at least offered the possibility of guiding the user through every activity where they might require, or at least desire, context and connection. The Web plus Google plus the smartphone means everyone can always be operating on the "best" information. We can always operate smarter – if we so choose. (Only in the second half of the 2010s – in an era of social media "engagement" and fake news – had the ideal of the "best" information become so clearly problematic.)

Google makes the Web searchable; a smartphone locates a user in space – via GPS and other sensors. Putting the two together offers a window into the world of metadata connected to place. At the end of the 2010s, this meant the world as viewed through Google's Maps or Earth products – or equivalent products from Apple, Nokia spin-out Here, and a few others. Providing locative data sets *in situ*, they offer up only a tiny window into the information that has been collected about the world. A tool like Google Maps might provide some basic information about a business (such as its hours of operation), filtering out all of the other metadata available about that location – because that narrow view serves the commercial purposes of the provider, rather than the potential needs of the user. Google's view onto the world serves its users only insofar as it serves Google's revenue stream.

Such a lens hides more than it reveals, and gives no hints about how much data lies behind it, nor how much could be revealed. Instead, user expectations about what can be known about the world – its locative metadata – have been conditioned by years of an experience of a few paltry crumbs, grudgingly proffered, from a very rich table of metadata. Users don't think about the world as data-laden and locatively meaningful precisely because no app has ever presented it in this way.

If a tool could clarify that view, sweeping comprehensively through these locative data sets, taking in everything known about a space, from within that space, and in the natural, locative context of that space, everything would suddenly become visibly impregnated with context and meaning. The world and its ghostly twin of locative metadata would resolve into focus, revealing a hidden and heretofore invisible digital depth.

This crucial connection between location and locative metadata – revealed in the pivotal moment of *Free Guy* – completely transforms our relationship to the world. Reading the world's metadata changes our experience

Reading the world's metadata changes our experience of the world.

of the world. The world immediately becomes apprehensible. It speaks for itself, offering guidance, advice, and caution. It can shape the activities of the people at a given location – and can do so selectively. The introductory example of Peg Paterson Park shows how the locative metadata within *Pokémon Go* acted to lure players to a location, then shaped their behavior at that location. The world may be constructed from inanimate objects, but its digital double, composed of information, context, and metadata, can read our presence and respond to it.

One example of this will be familiar to anyone who owns a late-model automobile. The affordances offered by an automobile to tune its performance, or modify handling characteristics, have migrated from purely mechanical to electromechanical – therefore under the management of largely undocumented software and electronic tools available only to authorized repairers.[6] When a car breaks down, it must be taken in for professional repairs, because the owner has no understanding of its operations. In another example of a "body without organs," the engine of a vehicle often hides beneath a large plastic cover: There's nothing here you can fix, so why even see it?

This modern automobile typifies a world which seeks to hide its complexities and the specificities of its operation behind a smooth façade.[7] Such façades empower their creators as bearers of hidden knowledge, while simultaneously disempowering owners, a theft of agency repeated countless times in the recent history of technology. Personal computers took 40 years to evolve from "homebrew" hand-assembled gadgets into machine-assembled and internally annealed slabs of silicon and plastic. Smartphones inherited the assembly techniques of the late-period PCs, never giving away any secrets of their operation or repair – something that has become true for much of our technical apparatus. Some of this can be attributed to cost-efficiencies in design and mass production, and rather more to the protection of intellectual property, but it always comes with a shift in the power relationship between producer and consumer. It represents a form of informational arbitrage, allowing parties with information to exploit the ignorance of those who lack it. The cost of this arbitrage revealed itself during the height of the 2020 COVID-19 pandemic: As global supply chains collapsed, it became impossible to repair or augment supplies of medical ventilators at a moment of greatest need for them – leading some nations to develop a local manufacturing capacity to meet their needs.

Metadata can be easily hidden via digitization, conferring power on those who can see it. The automobile, with no touchpoints beyond the few meted out by the manufacturer, can be operated by its owner, but in no sense can it be known by them. The authorized dealer – empowered by the manufacturer with some of the informational keys to the kingdom – has a degree of access that clearly prescribes permitted repair activities: That which cannot be seen cannot be fixed. The manufacturer sees everything: The entire history of the vehicle, from its initial product plans, to its design prototypes, engineering specifications, mechanical and manufacturing designs, even the design of the production lines for all of its components.

Yet even this huge vault of information – automobile metadata – barely scratches the surface.

Each instance of an automobile, and each instance of every component within an automobile, bears its own history of manufacture, shipping, and assembly, a chain of custody especially important when a defect has been detected, or a vehicle recall is made. The automobile manufacturer maintains all of this metadata about the physical basis for an automobile; for liability, so they can have insight into their own manufacturing processes, and so they can better manage manufacturing supply chains. A single bolt on an automobile carries with it an almost inconceivable depth of metadata: Pregnant with meaning, yet hidden and silent.[8]

The automobile manufacturer might question whether any of this metadata would be relevant to the owner, conjuring a dichotomy between the physical nature of an object and its metadata, *insisting that a physical object can be separated from its metadata*. In practice, the physical amounts to less than half of the object; without metadata, the object remains poorly known, and incomplete. That world tells us very little about itself, reserving its interiority for the empowered.

The first commercial successes in augmented reality leverage this empowerment via the revelation of metadata. A worker on a production line can use an AR display to see "into" a product during assembly; an engineer can tweak the specifications of a component during design; a technician can understand the manufacturing and operational history of an element under repair.[9] In each case, the addition of digital depth renders a previously opaque operation transparent and concise. Under the guidance of metadata, actions become obvious.

Augmented reality shapes human behavior in space. This congruence between metadata and operation makes individuals vastly more effective. As if sight had suddenly been restored to them, the augmented user inspects metadata, seeing what needs to be done, then does it quickly and effectively. That step-change delivered by augmentation becomes an incentive, broadening the scope and take-up of augmented reality throughout organizations, because greater augmentation means greater productivity.

Each application of augmentation requires its own set of metadata. Following the resolution of the engineering challenges associated with mass production of AR mirrorshades, much of the work in augmented reality over the next decades will focus on shaping metadata, so that it can best shape the activities of those using it. That metadata exists, but largely outside of any locative or operational contexts. The augmented worker needs metadata in context to operate at peak efficiency, something understood clearly in theory, but only dimly in practice.

Half a century of research in human–computer interaction informs the development of augmented reality interfaces, but the effective design of metadata in space will likely require years – possibly even decades – of development. Uniting the informational space of the Web with real-world, augmented reality resets the clock on computing as a design science. The informational connection between human, computer, and space requires new sensitivities and sensibilities, defining a "great project" for mid-twenty-first-century pioneers of computing, just as the basics of human–computer interaction defined research aims across the latter half of the twentieth century.

Even modestly effective marriages of metadata and space produce convincing results. Almost all uses of augmented reality lead to an increased demand for locative metadata, available within augmented reality. Use increases productivity, and productivity increases lead to increased use. As happened in the 1990s with the World Wide Web, and in the 2010s with the smartphone, this cycle of amplifying value creation acts as a lever to pry private and protected metadata from its hiding places, because of its greater value as a connected and contextualized resource than its value as informational arbitrage. Knowing more about space creates greater opportunity than sitting on metadata: A resource shared is a resource squared.[10] For businesses, the allure will be immediate and difficult to resist; the more they augment space, the greater their desire to augment space.

For an automobile manufacturer, the automobile-as-object rapidly evolves into a dense and deeply layered field of metadata interpenetrating the physical and computational structures of the vehicle. Every part possesses its own interiority, expressed as metadata, as does the vehicle as a whole, and each system within the vehicle, etc. No longer simply an object, in its full realization the automobile becomes a nexus of material, manufacture, history, and design, all inhabiting the same space.

This same will hold true for every object in the world. Some objects have intense, dense interiority, particularly those that have been touched most intensively by human activities. Others have little to say. Yet it seems unlikely that any part of the world will have nothing to say about itself: A lack of metadata speaks volumes – about privacy, or security, and agency. "Whereof one cannot speak, thereof one must be silent."[11]

The augmentation of reality expresses itself as an unexpected, ubiquitous, and profound deepening of our awareness of what the world says about itself. Our experience of the world rapidly transitions away from one framed by our own interiority – what we know about the world – to a relational frame, where our beliefs about the world can be mediated (even challenged) by what the world knows about itself. The narcissistic injuries of a world awakened by locative metadata will be continual, as the world speaks for itself, and against our needs. Just as we must confront the needs and wants of other humans when within the public sphere, so we will contend with the demands of the world, including the burden of knowing that the world knows.

Our theories of mind – how we imagine others think, and think about us – will extend to the content of the world itself. What does the world know? What does the world know about us? What does the world think it knows about us? In an age of surveillance capitalism these questions can never be ignored, because all connected devices can become mechanisms of betrayal. In an age of augmentation, our view of the world veers toward a post-scientific Animism; the world – in all of its individual elements – has interiority, agency, and feelings, both about itself and about us.[12]

111

Our world generated 2,500,000,000,000,000,000 bytes of data each day in 2018, a figure that continues to grow exponentially. Even if just one-millionth of this total represented locative metadata that could be observed by augmented reality users (a very conservative estimate), our information systems have already created trillions of elements of locative metadata, every single day.

This accelerating accumulation of locative data (as a subset of data generally) means that the view through all AR systems – even those that already exist, whether head-mounted or smartphone-based – onto any point within the world presents so much metadata that it becomes impossible to resolve anything specifically. Crowded together, too much meaning looks like noise. The world, over-inscribed, disappears completely, and the utility of locative metadata drowns within a sea of itself.

This has happened before; the human collation and curation of the Web by Yahoo! drowned in a rising tide of pages, links, and media.[13] However granular the subject area, every category within Yahoo! encompassed so much content that it became a useless, worthless distinction. While good with small lists and tight curation, human cognitive capacities quickly get overwhelmed, and too much quickly becomes just as worthless as nothing at all.

Hearing the world speak clearly within the cacophony of its metadata requires a capacity for tuned listening, a skill we do not possess innately, and therefore – as before, with the Web – we must delegate it to machines. AltaVista offered a free-text search of the Web; Google added the metadata of context and popularity. Each algorithm filtered the overwhelming quantity of Web content into a tiny, manageable trickle of information, and without them the Web would not be useable – except by other machines.

Web search engines transform text into a query, and submit that query as input into another algorithm, which replies with a set of responses – "hits." The equivalent process for locative metadata transforms a location into a query. This location could be absolute, such as in GPS coordinates, or relative to a greater whole, for example referring to a specific bolt on an engine block within an automobile. This location query returns the entire set of locative metadata about a place or an object or a specific instance of an object – and, quite possibly, all of these simultaneously. That will likely be a substantial set of locative metadata, meaning every query returns far more noise than signal.

Google built a trillion-dollar empire upon their capacity to filter the Web down to human scale.[14] Something similar will be required to provide the benefits of augmented reality in a way that guides its users with the insights they need, rather than the insights the world forces upon them. This always presents users with a dilemma; filters inevitably reflect and reinforce the biases of both their creators (likely commercial and driven to satisfy business imperatives) and their users. The "filter bubble" created by the smooth operation of a Web search engine like Google both helps users get things done, while simultaneously leaving them blind to the richness, complexity, and contradictions of the wider world.[15] We can already see this in operation:

Google filters much of the richness of its locative data set out of Google Maps, to satisfy its own needs.

Avoiding the worst elements of the filter bubble requires a reframing: Users do not search locative metadata, *they explore it*. An explorer has an interest in everything, from the grand to the tiny, local and global, and all scales in between, often having no idea what they're on the trail of until they're well into the pursuit. Insofar as they can, explorers operate without preconceptions, taking everything in, using curiosity and experience as guides.

Yet these explorers of locative metadata cannot operate alone. They need tools to help them sift meaning, to identify and classify and develop their window onto this world. These tools must operate in conjunction with the user, listening to them, mirroring them, observing them, and responding to them, in a dance of responsiveness that brings what we've already learned about human–computer interaction into this new medium.

Using the wealth of sensory data generated by AR users, tools will know a user's gaze direction, understand and interpret voice commands, and read the data stream generated by any cameras, using sophisticated pattern recognition to identify objects. All of this will help these tools to filter away the noise, giving the explorer a "clearer" view into the augmented world. Alongside the organization and presentation of locative metadata – and driven by it – such tools represent another of the "grand challenges" of twenty-first-century computing. Without such tools, the world of locative metadata will continually overwhelm its users, consigning it to the operations of machines that can be programmed to be algorithmically ignorant of the complexities that confound us.

As these tools learn from their interactions with users, profiling those users, they will require little user training, and will enable a legion of explorers. Just as the Web empowered billions with the capacity to have the best possible information at hand and on demand, these tools offer a world of locative metadata that continuously guides explorers through whatever view onto the world they deem most meaningful at that point in time. A world offering guidance shapes the behaviors of the people within it. Explorers of locative metadata will do as directed – or at least will always have that advice to refer to.

These tools shape more than the thoughts of the explorers of locative metadata; they shape their actions. Just as a rat will scamper along the walls of a maze in search of cheese, these tools can frame roadblocks and rewards to direct users toward goals. That makes these tools both incredibly potent and, for that reason, incredibly valuable, and this requires that such tools must be entirely transparent in their construction, operation, and underlying data sources. "First we shape our tools, thereafter our tools shape us."[16]

The potential increase in human capacity accompanying a fully realized and explorable world of locative metadata could make the Web seem as though just a prelude to the main act. Within a generation, the Web could be considered merely a confining and self-referential space of human concerns, paling into insignificance against the universe of the real. That real world – or, at least, those windows onto the real afforded by our tools – needs to speak to us, engage us, and, through its infinity of voices, move us to consider its own significance, agency, and immanence. It will soon do so – though we may not always appreciate what it has to say.

As our world reveals a new interiority of locative metadata, it becomes of paramount importance to consider who makes these contributions. Where the whole world has become the Web, and the Web the whole world, and the world seems to speak for itself, we must always ask "Who speaks for the world?"

The potential increase in human capacity accompanying a fully realized and explorable world of locative metadata could make the Web seem as though just a prelude to the main act.

5
Setting the World to Writes

In the future, I think that more of us are going to contribute to culture and society in ways that are not measured by traditional economics and GDP. All of us are going to do what today is considered the arts, and that's going to form the basis of a lot of our communities.

A philosopher – or social leader – waxing optimistic about a less materialistic culture for the mid-twenty-first century?

That's why I'm so excited about augmented reality, because it's going to make it so that we can create all kinds of things that until today have only been possible in the digital world, and we're gonna be able to interact with them and explore them together.

Perhaps not a social leader – but a technological visionary, promising a bright tomorrow?

So at last year's F8, we talked about our 10-year roadmap to give everyone in the world the power to share anything they want, with anyone. And one of the key long-term technologies that we talked about is augmented reality.

On April 18, 2017, Facebook founder and CEO Mark Zuckerberg fronted a few thousand engineers and designers at the firm's annual F8 ("fate") conference, introducing augmented reality as something that – although it might be important to Facebook – would be far more important to the world.[1]

Now, we all know where we want this to get eventually, right, we want glasses, or eventually contact lenses that look and feel normal. But let us overlay all kinds of information and digital objects on top of the real world.

So we can just be sitting here and we want to play chess, snap, here's a chess board, and we can play together.

Zuckerberg understands that changing space changes the behavior of people within that space. Magic up a chessboard and people begin to play chess.

Or you want to watch TV, we can put a digital TV on that wall. And instead of being a piece of hardware, it's a $1 app instead of a $500 piece of equipment.

Here Zuckerberg seems to gloss over a salient fact: His $1 TV app runs on a several thousand dollar and yet-to-be-mass-produced piece of Facebook hardware – AR mirrorshades.

So think about how many of the things that we have in our lives actually don't need to be physical – that can be digital – and think about how much better and more affordable and accessible they're going to be when they are.

Instead of the promised world of artistic post-materiality, this sounds like a materialist paradise. But Zuckerberg offered more than the satisfactions of pseudo-materiality; he offered a peek into the hidden world of locative metadata:

Think about going to Rome on vacation and having information about the Colosseum overlaid on the actual building or directions overlaid on the actual street.

In the real world, metadata provides guidance and context, but augmented reality has another capacity: It can overwrite the real.

And think about if your daughter is a big Harry Potter fan. For her birthday, you can change your home into Hogwarts.

That magical translation of imagination into reality illustrates the power of augmented reality. Yet, as Zuckerberg acknowledges – in a throw-away line to his audience – imagination need not be benign:

Although I bet some of you were hoping I'd hit the toilet paper button.

Nine months after the massive global success of *Pokémon*

Go, Zuckerberg's speech amounted to a "coming out party" for augmented reality. As Zuckerberg laid out the goals, capacities, and potentials of a medium still very young and raw, Facebook took its first public steps toward its long-term vision[2] as a provider and curator of a new type of consensus reality:

> We see the beginning of a new platform.
>
> We're not using primitive tools today because we prefer primitive tools. We're using primitive tools, because we're still early in the journey to create better ones.
>
> And in order to create better tools, first, we need an open platform where any developer in the world can build for augmented reality without having to first build their own camera and get a lot of people to use it. But when you look around at all the different cameras that are out there today, no one has built the platform yet. So today, we're going to start building this platform together. And we're going to make the camera the first mainstream augmented reality platform.

Within its ubiquitously installed Facebook app, Zuckerberg promised to deliver sophisticated augmented reality capabilities, driven by the smartphone camera:

> For those of you who watched us roll out cameras across all our apps, and you wondered what we might have been doing – that was act one. This is act two: giving developers the power to build for augmented reality in the first augmented reality platform, the camera.

Just as Google Cardboard proved that smartphones

offered everything needed to deliver credible virtual reality experiences, *Pokémon Go* proved that smartphones already offered enough sensors to deliver a credible augmented reality environment – using SLAM:

> You need to have a platform that gives them precise location or realistic relationship with objects around them in their environment.
>
> So there's an AI technique for doing this, called simultaneous localization and mapping – or SLAM.

And once you have the Facebook app, with its smartphone-sensor-enabled SLAM capabilities, the entire world becomes a palimpsest:

> And here's how this works: You're gonna be able to easily create anything you want. You can write a fun message next to breakfast and you're going to be able to slide it onto the table ... And you're going to pan around and it's going to maintain its position on the table exactly as if it were a real object in the world.

Zuckerberg's demo shows developers that this new platform will make the hard parts of augmented reality – such as SLAM – a breeze.

Circling back to the lofty ideals expressed in his opening comments, Zuckerberg gives a demo of a future filled with augmented reality art:

> Let's talk about art.
>
> Now with augmented reality, you're going to be able to create and discover all kinds of new art around your city.

This is actually a piece at Facebook headquarters: Without augmented reality, this actually just looks like a blank wall, but when you are in augmented reality, you get this beautiful piece of art.

That's not just a painting on the wall, but it fills up the whole space. It's 3D. Not only that: it's something that would be impossible to build, or make in reality, because you have this infinite waterfall of paint coming down. It's really quite something to look at.

Now, one thing that's kind of a funny side effect of this is that now we're on Facebook, we noticed that they're just people gathering around looking at blank walls.

This is going to be a thing in the future.

These "blank walls" have been inscribed with locative metadata; Facebook's app renders that metadata visible. But who created this metadata? How did they "publish" this metadata to make it accessible via the Facebook app? And who can see it? Would it be visible to everyone – or just those who paid for a privileged view? And whose wall, whose space, whose things have been inscribed?

None of these questions seems particularly relevant in the example of a trifling bit of animated wall art. Everything that Zuckerberg used in his pleasant, culturally sensitive examples pointed away from the implications of being able to inscribe and render locative metadata upon any surface in the world.

Leaving art behind, he quickly brings the demo back to world-as-palimpsest:

Now, one of the things that I've always wanted to do is leave notes for friends at different places.

123

In order to do this, you need to have a really precise sense of location.

This isn't just about finding a Pokémon within a one block radius – you need a very exact location. I'm talking about sharing a note to tell your friend what the best special is – right next to the sign of the specials at a restaurant. Or marking your table at the local dive bar that you go to with your friends. Or leaving a note for your wife on the refrigerator.

Some of this stuff is going to be really special.

Social media connects and unites, making it easy to "find the others," the like-minded who share interests, activities – and beliefs.[3] Connecting and uniting around beliefs tends to reinforce those beliefs. Individuals, rewarded by the group for orthodoxy, avoid heterodox expressions within themselves, and, via the psycho-analytic "Shadow" (those repressed expressions, ruminating), come to hate others who embody any difference. Within the group, that hatred takes form as exposure and expulsion from the group – a common-place of human behavior for every cult of believers going as far back as we have written records: Shunning, exile, and, of course, burnings.

Where one group as a whole identifies an individual or another group as heterodox, there that group discovers it can weaponize its newfound connectivity, and goes to war. "Flame wars" during the Internet's earliest days repeatedly saw minor differences amplified, hardening into ideological positions – confirmation of the recent discovery by cognitive psychologists that confronting an individual's beliefs tends to fix them.

By the mid-2000s, the Internet had scaled up to hundreds of millions of users. Self-selecting long before they underwent any process of self-identification, many communities of believers acted together as a subcultural group before they recognized their uniqueness. They read the same articles – and shared them. They watched the same films – and critiqued them. They played the same video games.

In 2014, a global community of gamers, connected through websites such as 4chan and Reddit, found their *axis mundi* in a set of provably false accusations made about independent game developer Zoë Quinn.[4] The controversy, shared widely across social media, recapitulated the right-versus-left "culture wars." In a hyper-connected medium, however, believers could fan the flames of passion, sharing information, speculation, and confabulation in a stew of anger, hatred, and defiance. "Gamergate" saw Zoë Quinn harassed, threatened, "doxed" (through the widespread release of personal details such as her address and phone number), and hounded into hiding. These newly self-described "Gamergators" saw themselves as the righteous, poorly done by, but now activated by the medium that had brought them together, using every means at their disposal against the despised Other, so-called "social justice warriors."

Yet the conflict came to mean more than its causes. Tools and techniques assembled for the first time by Gamergators found their way into a broader toolkit, for a new sort of social policing. Being too public, too outspoken, or too heterodox risked attacks of the kind Quinn endured – particularly for women. "Doxing" evolved into "swatting," where police emergency response teams would be misdirected to a target's home or business, expecting to find a hostage situation, but instead confronting a very scared and confused individual – who might be accidentally shot by police.

Connection has always carried with it the menace of mob rule. After Gamergate, that became impossible to ignore. Connected, any community could suddenly shift, embrace its own shadow, and go on the warpath.

By the time of Zuckerberg's 2017 F8 keynote, Facebook already housed a broad range of communities of belief – everything from mainstream religions to cults to the uglier groupings of racism and authoritarianism. Bringing people together has always meant bringing out the worst in some of them; post-Gamergate, that could quickly lead to warfare by weaponized connectivity.

Though that point should have been obvious to a social media billionaire by 2017, Zuckerberg betrayed a nearly Pollyanna-ish view of how Facebook's potent new AR technology would be put to work by the network's billions of users. All of whom – judging by Zuckerberg's insouciant attitude – had the souls of saints.

Put art on a wall. Annotate a menu with your favorites. Leave a note for your wife. All of these very sweet, very reasonable, and very human desires for communication and connection conveniently overlook the darker side of human emotions – feelings such as anger, hatred, revenge. Feelings that we have learned how to engage, *en masse*, through social media.

Even if only one in a thousand Facebook users identify as "bad actors," that adds up to an army of two million marauders using augmented reality and locative metadata in ways its creators never intended. In a weaponized social media environment, safety requires an imagination of worst cases: Instead of art on a wall, a swastika on a synagogue;[5] instead of a review of a menu, an outrageous, unprovable slander against a business owned by an enemy; instead of a love note to a wife, the hideous, anonymous messages left by a stalker who reveals, by their placement, that the target of those messages has been under their surveillance.

Although it may appear unreasonable to reframe Zuckerberg's examples as extremes – Facebook would never condone such behaviors – the technology supports these usages and therefore they must be highlighted as possibilities *before* they become common. Augmented reality enables users to inscribe locative metadata upon the world: Who can say what they will write?

Precisely because of the potency of locative metadata, it will attract bad actors seeking its technological "hyperempowerment."[6] Hate speech, expressed within augmented reality, will bedevil the medium. Although social media platforms make attempts to police the hate speech posted to their platforms, such policing does not scale, requiring either a legion of human censors continually reviewing content, or a type of general artificial intelligence that has never yet been achieved, and still looks very far away.

In any case, such policing operates only on publicly accessible content. Private groups can share content freely amongst themselves, operating without the oversight of the censor. A racist or ethnonationalist group could freely inscribe locative metadata upon the world: Identifying immigrants, undesirables, and political enemies undetectably – except to the members of the group. They can do this because they've taken a tool generously provided by Facebook and turned it toward their own ends.

The providers of locative metadata systems – vast, networked data sets collectively known as the "AR cloud"[7] – will seek to remedy the worst of these excesses, perhaps prohibiting certain areas from being inscribed with locative metadata, and possibly even subjecting all locative metadata published through their AR clouds to a process of review. None of this will work – human beings are always craftier than any set of rules that seek to constrain their behaviors – and all of it asserts an astonishing new property right trumpeted during Zuckerberg's keynote, yet seemingly ignored by all: The right to inscribe locative metadata *anywhere*.

While Facebook obviously has the right to inscribe an augmented reality artwork onto the wall of its offices, why should its tools grant users the right to scribble something on a menu at a restaurant? If a patron took an indelible marker to the menu outside a restaurant, they would likely be cautioned, perhaps ejected from the establishment, possibly even subject to civil or criminal penalties. The inscription of locative metadata, seen by less sympathetic eyes than Mark Zuckerberg's, looks like graffiti, or vandalism. Such a position has nothing to do with intent, but with permission: *Do you have the right to write?*

The first substantial assertion of this "right to write" came from Niantic's AR smartphone game *Ingress*. Resting upon the data set of the world, *Ingress* players could read and write to Niantic's layer locative metadata without respect to or awareness of the legally entitled occupiers of that location. A public sculpture, inscribed as an *Ingress* portal, could become a battleground.

So could a public park.

That assertion of Niantic's ability to freely inscribe locative metadata on the world led to Peg Paterson Park in Rhodes filling with *Pokémon Go* players in July 2016. The residents and homeowners of Rhodes, confronted with a technologically coordinated mob, had no idea why their tiny public park had become such an alluring attraction. Niantic had acted as if it had every right to write locative metadata on Peg Paterson Park – without any thought for other stakeholders, such as the local council (legal owners of the park), neighbors, fire and safety officers, and so forth.[8]

This fundamentally extractive attitude – monetizing space through the inscription of locative metadata without respect to any other party's rights or their own responsibilities – typifies the data-driven business model for technology firms operating at global scale.[9] Facebook extracts value from its users' desire to share; Google from user searches, email communications, and travels. Yet the pretense of a value exchange could be made in defense of these examples: Facebook's users at least get the ability to publish – at the cost of their data and their privacy.

Where they remain unrecognized, locative metadata property rights are simply seized, for *the ability to inscribe locative metadata is a property right*. Locative metadata changes space, changing the behavior of people in that space, and thereby changes the value of that space: Clever café owners deployed *Pokémon Go* lures in their venues, driving street traffic into their shops and increasing sales.[10]

Just because Niantic (or Facebook, or any other AR cloud provider) implements a system to inscribe locative metadata, this does not automatically grant them the right to deploy it anywhere they choose. Capacity is necessary, but wholly insufficient. Capacity must be paired with permission; otherwise, those who have legal rights to a space – and, therefore, legal "writes" to a space – lose their ability to speak for the space. Instead, other voices, with other motives, speak for the space, a loss of control that could be as profound as the loss of rights to the space itself.

In bringing AR capabilities to the billions of users of its smartphone app, Facebook makes the world "writeable." Facebook's users freely inscribe their own locative metadata on the world, at will, without any acknowledgment of, or negotiation with, the rights of those who own or manage those spaces. The world becomes Facebook's palimpsest, losing its ability to speak for itself without Facebook also speaking for it.

To counter the many irritations, violations, and outrages that will obviously accumulate as these capacities end up in the hands of "bad actors," Facebook (and all the other AR clouds) will undoubtedly apologize – then offer the owners of affected spaces "privacy settings"[11] allowing them to manage how Facebook's users write locative metadata within their spaces.

Here the extractive strategy reaches its culmination: Having created this problem, Facebook could propose to manage it, by asking owners of space to let Facebook

The ability to inscribe locative metadata is a property right.

manage their locative metadata privacy rights, effectively handing Facebook the right to write that they never had any legitimate right to claim.

In the years following the release of *Pokémon Go*, multiple lawsuits filed against Niantic worked to define the property rights associated with locative metadata, and the damages associated with the violation of those rights. On February 15, 2019, *The Hollywood Reporter* ran an article titled "'Pokemon Go' Creator Agrees to Tighter Leash on Virtual Creatures to End Class Action":

> ... homeowners suing over the way that the augmented reality game *Pokémon Go* led players to congregate on or near private property submitted a proposed settlement ... creator Niantic will become much more legally responsible for the virtual creatures ... Although that might sound funny, the case itself had the potential of redefining "trespass" in the digital age.[12]

As can be seen in this first-in-the-world settlement, a rapidly evolving body of civil legal agreements represents a first pass at the new regulatory frameworks needed to managing locative metadata. As the world's digital twin reveals itself in its potency and value, it has attracted the eye of both courts and legislators. The revelation of a new property right carries with it far-reaching implications; the bulk of the law concerns commercial transactions, with an emphasis on property and property rights.

Prioritizing public safety, legislators will direct regulators to ensure that locative metadata cannot easily be abused. Although it may prove impossible to prevent all abuses, policing the providers of AR cloud services (likely only a handful will operate at global scale) seems a more achievable goal. These firms will need to be held accountable both for their actions, and the actions of their users. Heavy civil penalties should accompany violations of public interest and public safety, with criminal penalties available when those technologies have been weaponized and used as tools of assault. Setting the costs of non-compliance high tends to encourage "good enough" behavior.

A rough analogy can be found in the global regulatory frameworks forming around UAVs – unmanned aerial vehicles, or drones. After a number of near-miss encounters between drones and civil aircraft operating out of British airports, new regulations around the construction and operation of drones came into effect.[13] Drone manufacturers now embed a detailed set of location metadata into the drone's software, including a list of "no fly" zones, such as 3- to 5-kilometer rings around major airports. Additionally, drone pilots themselves must now be licensed in the UK (and in other domains such as Australia[14]) to operate drones above a certain vehicle weight and flight altitude. None of these new regulations completely precludes the operations of a "bad actor," someone who might modify firmware and ignore operating regulations in pursuit of their mischief – but it does make things substantially more difficult. After these protections have been voided, law enforcement has the permission to act – and the responsibility to protect public safety.

Just as airports and aeronautical regulators assert the right to control the flight space of UAVs, regulators could assert the right to write locative metadata. They must first claim this right for all public spaces, as trustees of those spaces. They can also claim a similar right over all private spaces, in their roles as regulator and arbiter. Where a private owner wishes to manage their own locative data rights, they should be free to do so. Where, for any reason, the private owner is unable or unwilling to manage those rights, regulators can backstop that lack of capacity with their own regulations and infrastructure. This would prevent such "fallow" spaces from quickly becoming the effective property of whatever commercial organization or social group decides to monetize their locative metadata.

Such a system would have its own rough analogy in the Domain Name System (DNS), the technology mapping a human-readable space of names to a machine-readable set of Internet addresses.[15] (Using DNS, the human-readable web location politypress.com maps onto the machine address 166.62.28.112.) DNS translates human language into access to computational resources at global scale.

Since its earliest days, DNS has been under the auspices of a self-constituted but globally recognized regulatory authority – The Internet Corporation for Assigned Names and Numbers (ICANN). Preventing multiple organizations from using the same names (confusing) or the same Internet addresses (dangerous, and a pathway to fraud), ICANN manages the "name space" of the Internet, allowing it to flourish without descending into chaos.

Serving a similar purpose, a hypothetical Internet Corporation for the Assignment of Locative Metadata, or ICALM, could allow the owners or authorized representatives of spaces to register those spaces across a globally accessible and verifiable registry, similar to the Domain Name System. Once assigned, the assignee then has full rights to control all locative metadata activities within that space (subject to local regulations).[16] Niantic could not site a portal or a Pokéstop at a location thus assigned without the explicit and continued permission of the assignee, nor could any Facebook user inscribe any locative metadata without permission.

Such a proposal would make the work of bad actors much harder, but this represents only a beginning. Power lies not only in being able to prevent the writing of locative metadata, but conversely, to limit the ability to read it. A space need not simply present itself as an open book that can be read by all comers. Instead, it should be able to say whatever it has judged appropriate, after a thorough inspection of the request and the requester. Space must always retain the option to remain silent.

This "right of silence" represents a freedom not envisaged by any of the AR cloud providers, each of whom assume that the whole of the world will be theirs to inscribe, and read as they will. Without private property there is no private life; without the protections of privacy afforded to locative metadata, there can be no private space. (Even so, silence speaks volumes; silence itself can be interpreted as a form of metadata – presence by absence.)

Where space speaks for itself, it must have at least the right to speak with an authoritative voice. It may not choose to do so, but that choice provides the agency that allows both readers and writers of locative metadata to have some sense of trust within an environment that could otherwise speak in ways that would deprive both of agency.

Who speaks for the world? Before AR cloud providers shrink that into a question of technological capability, we need to create organizations and institutions that maintain our existing systems of ownership – however flawed – because we can at least assert our agency within them, through legal means. Assigning the right to write to any commercial organization will only see them monetized, potentially weaponized, and reframed as technicalities, rather than consequential property rights, with the potential to shape human behavior.

All of these issues came to a head back in 2017, when social media company Snap created a marketing campaign to popularize the augmented reality features in their own smartphone app. A fierce competitor of Facebook (famously rebuffing a multi-billion-dollar offer to purchase the startup), Snap built camera-driven SLAM features into its app, so that its users could add their own AR effects to their social video messages. To promote those features, Snap drafted a number of globally famous artists to create works visible through their app. As *Variety* reported on October 3, 2017:

> Snap CEO Evan Spiegel used the stage at the 2017 Vanity Fair New Establishment Summit to announce a collaboration with Jeff Koons ... Starting Tuesday, the art exhibits will show up for Snapchat users in major parks and landmarks ... current live locations for the

136

Koons installations [include] New York City's Central Park.

The article does not report on whether New York City officials had been notified of Snap's decision to locate Koon's 5-meter-high "Balloon Dog" artwork in the middle of Central Park. The right to write had not been identified in 2017; Snap simply acted as though they had every right to inscribe their own metadata onto New York's most famous and beloved public space.

Although some members of the public delighted in an installation of Koon's "Balloon Dog," Brooklyn-based artist Sebastian ErraZuriz immediately recognized it as a violation and colonization of public space, crafting an intervention to make that abundantly clear. From *Mashable*, October 5, 2017:

> On Wednesday New York-based artist Sebastian Errazuriz and his studio Cross Lab protested Snapchat's latest attempt to woo users by vandalizing Koons' Balloon Dog installation, which appears on the app in Central Park ... The final result? A graffiti-bombed version of the AR sculpture, which Errazuriz geo-tagged as the exact same GPS coordinates as Snapchat's version. Game on.

In the early 1960s, Marshall McLuhan noted that artists operate as early warning systems for culture, with their eyes fixed on the present – while everyone else gazes into the rear-view mirror.

ErraZuriz saw through this experiment in AR art – a private reality for Snap's members, yet occupying public space – using his graffiti attack to draw attention to Snap's appropriation of public space, monetizing it for marketing, branding, and advertising. Snap carefully protects its own AR cloud, so while ErraZuriz could not "tag" the Snap version of Balloon Dog, he drew attention to the way Snap asserted the right to write. By doing that, ErraZuriz provided an early warning of what the right to write – and its opposite – looks like.

As augmented reality grows more common, we need to ensure that we can be secure in our own spaces, without fear of being written out of the story the world tells about itself and about us. To do that, we cannot simply rely on the good graces of businesses busily seeking to monetize space. Instead, we must act together, through a mix of governmental, legal, regulatory, and standardization mechanisms. Only when all of these have been engaged in concert – regionally, nationally, and internationally – do they present enough of a barrier to the interests of multiple trillion-dollar entities. We must hang together on this, lest we be divided and conquered. The right to write, in its concise expression, is the right to own – or to be owned. If we do not want to be owned, we must protect our writes.

As augmented reality grows more common, we need to ensure that we can be secure in our own spaces, without fear of being written out of the story the world tells about itself and about us.

Conclusion: No Feint but What We Make

On a Christmas morning not too many years from now, you unwrap a small and long-awaited present. The box, emblazoned with a famous logo, opens easily, revealing a pair of white-rimmed spectacles. Putting them on, you're guided through a brief setup procedure – conversationally, as these spectacles can listen to you, and respond to you in authoritative feminine tones. These spectacles first calibrate to your eyes, then connect to your mobile, and, once you've provided your username and password – log you into the cloud.

Everything you see suddenly transforms.

Looking around the room, cameras on those spectacles scan the contours of the space, resolving shape and color, uploading all of that to the cloud, which performs algorithmic pattern matching against a data set of tens of millions of objects. As the cloud recognizes objects, it sends back relevant information, showing up in your spectacles: Above, around, or within those objects.

Within a few moments, your entire space pulses with information that you can reach out toward, dive into, and explore.

Everything appears to have something to say; the various connected devices chirp and jabber and seem very busy, while the lamps and the walls and even the Christmas tree also have information within them – things you never knew, and certainly never suspected that they knew about themselves. You can immediately see that your smartphone currently feeds a vast stream of data into the cloud; that a CFL (compact fluorescent lamp) bulb in a ceiling fixture will soon burn out; that the Christmas tree needs a good watering.

It's delightful and magical and (though you'd only admit this privately) perhaps a bit overwhelming. You wish you had a control that might let you "dial things back," to a more comfortable density of intensity. But you resolve to get used to it. You begin to realize the trick lies in choosing what to ignore, and what to focus on. In the beginning, everything appears interesting, but – within a few hours – you learn that where you look, and what you look at, modulates the depth of information that you experience. Stare deeply into something, and it reveals its data like a flower blossoming. Quickly glance over something and it stays quiet. Okay, you think, this might work out.

Later in the day you go out for a stroll. The world breathes with information: This home – private, its information hidden. That business – closed today for the holiday, but open tomorrow at 7a.m. for the post-holiday sales, here's an advertisement of what you can buy! A park, with facilities highlighted with arrows, and a calendar of upcoming events, with an interesting tree – rare, carefully tended, and favored by a certain species of bee. All of it says something, and you can feel the press of all of the world's information: What should you consider? What can you ignore? How can you know?

Suddenly, some text appears at the lower left-hand corner of the display: "User profiling complete, begin curation?" Curation sounds useful – perhaps it could help to tame this riot of meaning? You bark a curt "Begin curation!" and everything ... gently ... mellows. Density melts away, replaced by a softer, ambient glow. Things have meaning, but that meaning remains indistinct, hovering on the edge of visibility. The cloud now decides for you what has immediate meaning, and how hard you'll need to look into something before it reveals its depths of information. You feel cradled within this new world, rather than tossed about by it.

At the end of the day, preparing for sleep, you finally remove your new spectacles. The world as it once was returns. It now feels weirdly empty and soulless, as though missing something essential – and immanent. So you slip those spectacles on, one more time, just to reassure yourself that this new world is more than just a dream. It will be there tomorrow, and forever after.

* * *

In our mind's eyes we can dream up fantastic worlds of paradise and delight – and hell and terror. We want to believe in utopias, but we live in a world that always falls far short of its promises. The magic within our

142

minds smooths the gaps in our experience, relying on imagination to endure the specific, disappointing, and unfulfilled, using our gifts to conjure another reality: Close to this one, but better.

More than half a century ago, Ivan Sutherland hypothesized an "Ultimate Display," offering an Alice-in-Wonderland window into a synthetic world. His "Sword of Damocles" brought computers together with humans in a deep, sensual union, an alchemical marriage of information and sensation known today as augmented reality. A true genius, Sutherland gave the world a technology it could fully understand, yet so difficult to achieve that it took on the glamour of a tantalizing, ultimate goal. The imagination of that ultimate display shaped the course of twentieth- and twenty-first-century computing.

Augmented reality allows us to seamlessly blend the synthetic and the real. It allows us to curate reality; adding that which pleases us, editing out that which does not. Yet because it presents us with ultimate control of the real, an ultimate display comes with some significant – and fundamental – cautions.

First among these centers on augmented reality as a technology of surveillance. Sensors and surveillance make augmented reality possible, translating the shape of a space into information, along with the location and the orientation of the human body, so that the mind can be algorithmically manipulated. Synthesizing reality requires a detailed awareness of reality.

Surveillance always raises the question of who watches – and who watches the watchmen? By itself, no augmented reality system knows enough about the world to offer more than some very simple modifications to the real. Instead, augmented reality systems need to function as one element within a much larger assemblage of networks and computational resources – and networked actors.

In this sense, all augmented reality systems serve as the displays of a single, vast global computer. This global computer manages the synthesis of reality for its users. In order to do this, that global computer requires an accurate stream of sensor and surveillance data from every user's system. This means that augmented reality systems serve as surveillance points for these global computers. Generating a synthetic reality for the users of these augmented reality systems requires a continuous stream of highly specific, meaningful, and valuable data from those users, data that will inevitably end up deposited with the usual suspects: Facebook, Google, Microsoft, Apple, plus their equivalents in China.

The evolution of the Web from universal information resource into a sort of super-sticky "flypaper for human attention" shows how this stream of user data can be used to profile those users. Using a combination of measurement and testing, profile data can be fed back to users to increase their "engagement." Augmented reality inherits all of the history and technology of the Web: This means these devices can profile their users as part of their operation. That profiling data can be used to make continual, progressive changes – framed as improvements – in the synthetic reality delivered to a user, in order to increase their engagement. What user would not prefer a better world?

144

Conclusion: No Feint but What We Make

"Information is a name for the content of what is exchanged with the outer world as we adjust to it, and make our adjustment felt upon it." When Norbert Wiener wrote these lines in *The Human Use of Human Beings*, he highlighted the power relationship between information and human experience – and tried to warn us that where content can be measured precisely, and adjusted algorithmically, *information makes that adjustment to us.*

Steering clear of the dystopian potential of augmented reality – a world where the technology turns humanity into managed, "dumb terminals" whose agency has been thwarted through profiling and "engagement" – requires both critical engagement with the medium as it emerges, and a willingness to undermine and expose its operations. Asking "who profits?" in an era of global-scale networked technology requires an understanding of the systemic nature of augmented reality systems. Neither device nor network nor application nor content, augmented reality emerges from the intersection of all of these – connected via global capital. All must be considered together; a failure to understand or detail any one of them creates a vulnerability through which human agency could be spirited away.

The counterweight to all of this horror comes in a new revelation of the world, as its digital twin finds a voice with which it can speak for itself. Although augmented reality promises unbounded imagination, it brings its greatest value to the material of reality. A formerly silent material world can now announce itself, its agency and intention. Locative metadata means that the world can be its own guide – both for itself and

145

for us. Where humanity has always moved through the world blindly unaware of it, this world can now loudly proclaim its information, opportunity – and resistance. We can learn much from the world, and be guided by it, but we will also contend with its new agency. For a species that regards itself as the singular possessor of that agency, this will take some getting used to.

Finally, we must ask, "Who speaks for the world?" Locative metadata resides within global-scale AR clouds – owned by the usual suspects. The owners of these technological systems have already begun to assert that this grants them a new property right – the "right to write" locative metadata. They act at present as though this right to write can be used without permission of the property owner. Yet changing space changes the behavior of people in that space, and thereby changes the value of that space. If unchallenged by property owners – currently perhaps only dimly aware of this potential theft of a property right via a bit of techno-logical sleight of hand – these trillion-dollar tech giants can act as though all of the real world belongs to them, to be inscribed with locative metadata serving their own ends.

Countering this attempted colonization of the world's digital twin requires community, institutional, and, ultimately, political responses. The Internet and the Web developed such responses before they had accumu-lated significant value. With trillions of dollars of capital on the line – and the prize nothing less than the control of reality – the battle over the "right to write" promises to be long, intense, and ugly. Those economic interests could well press their case until the bitter end,

With trillions of dollars of capital on the line, the battle over the "right to write" promises to be long, intense, and ugly.

focused on one goal: Gaining private control over how we inscribe the real. In the years ahead, we must always remember that who writes our world also writes us.

Technologies that couple to the mind at scale have already proven problematic, even terrifying. Fifty years ago, Ivan Sutherland dreamed of easy-to-use computers; we got them – and intensive user profiling. Twenty years ago, we wanted responsive websites; with them came "engagement" and addiction. Today we want augmented reality; let us hope that, in our ignorance, we do not give birth to the ultimate tool of surveillance, profiling, and control.

We must do more than hope. We must work toward the world we want to see, and do that before the world unboxes this latest gift from Pandora. The path we walk at present represents the consequences of all the decisions we have already made. We can learn from that past, and perhaps avoid its pitfalls. If we have hopes for the future, first among these must be that its problems are unique. As we continue our walk, we must never forget that all technologies contain within them dilemmas inherent to their nature. You cannot solve a dilemma; you can only endure it. In order to seize the prize, we must pay the price.

Notes

Introduction: A Riot in Rhodes

1 Zorine Te, "How Pokemon Go Nearly Destroyed a Quiet Suburb," Gamespot, August 2, 2016, https://www.gamespot.com/articles/how-pokemon-go-nearly-destroyed-a-quiet-suburb/1100-6442283/

2 James Lemon, "Pokemon Go: Residents call police as Rhodes swamped," *Sydney Morning Herald*, July 13, 2016, https://www.smh.com.au/business/consumer-affairs/pokemon-go-residents-call-police-as-rhodes-swamped-20160713-gq4hb3.html

3 Kathryn Wicks, "Pokemon GO: All Pokestops removed from Peg Paterson Park at Rhodes," *Sydney Morning Herald*, August 1, 2016, https://www.smh.com.au/technology/pokemon-go-all-pokestops-removed-from-peg-paterson-park-at-rhodes-20160801-gqio00.html

4 Ian Bogost, "Every Place Is Exactly the Same Now," *The Atlantic*, January 16, 2020, https://www.theatlantic.com/technology/archive/2020/01/smartphone-has-ruined-space/605077/

5 Franziska Roesner, "Who Is Thinking About Security and Privacy for Augmented Reality?," *Technology Review*, October 19, 2017, https://www.technologyreview.com/s/609143/who-is-thinking-about-security-and-privacy-for-augmented-reality/

6 Marshall McLuhan, *Understanding Media: The Extensions of Man* (New York: McGraw-Hill, 1964), pp. 119–30.

7 William Gibson, "The Shape of Things to Come," *The Economist*, December 4, 2003.

Chapter 1: The Will to Empower

1 Claus Pias, ed., *The Macy Conferences 1946–1953. The Complete Transactions* (Chicago: University of Chicago Press, 2016).

2 Norbert Wiener, *Cybernetics: or Control and Communication in the Animal and the Machine*, 2nd edn (Cambridge, MA: MIT Press, 1965).

3 Norbert Wiener, *The Human Use of Human Beings: Cybernetics and Society* (New York: Houghton Mifflin, 1954), p. 17.

4 Mitchel Waldrop, *The Dream Machine: J.C.R. Licklider and the Revolution that Made Computing Personal* (New York: Viking, 2001), pp. 101–5.

5 Ibid., pp. 117–21.

6 J. C. R. Licklider, "Man-Computer Symbiosis," *IRE Transactions on Human Factors in Electronics*, HFE-1, March 1960, pp. 4–11.

7 Waldrop, *The Dream Machine*, pp. 201–58.

8 Ibid., p. 255.

9 Ibid., p. 256.
10 Ivan Sutherland, "The Ultimate Display," Information Processing Technologies Office, ARPA, OSD, 1965.
11 Ivan Sutherland, "A Head Mounted Three Dimensional Display," AIFPS Fall Joint Computer Conference Proceedings, December 1968.
12 Howard Rheingold, *Virtual Reality* (New York: Summit Books, 1991), pp. 147–9.
13 Privately reported to the author.
14 Wikipedia, "Helmet-mounted Display," https://en.wikipedia.org/wiki/Helmet-mounted_display#Integrated_Helmet_And_Display_Sight_System_(IHADSS)
15 Paul Miller, "Microsoft Kinect Revealed: Project Natal Finally Gets a Name," Engadget, June 13, 2010, https://www.engadget.com/2010/06/13/microsoft-kinect-revealed-project-natal-finally-gets-a-name/
16 J. P. Gowdner, "Apple Purchases PrimeSense, Opening Up New Computing Experiences – And Enterprise Solutions," Forbes, November 25, 2013, https://www.forbes.com/sites/forrester/2013/11/25/apple-purchases-primesense-opening-up-new-computing-experiences-and-enterprise-solutions/#4e3b9e830706
17 R. Buckminster Fuller, *Critical Path* (New York: St Martin's Press, 1981), pp. 198–208.
18 Online news roundup, *Wall Street Journal*, October 27, 2004, https://www.wsj.com/articles/SB109888284313557107
19 McLuhan, *Understanding Media*, pp. 48–55.
20 Mark Bergen, "Why Did Google Get Rid of the Company Behind Pokémon Go?," Vox Recode,

July 12, 2016, https://www.vox.com/2016/7/12/12153722/google-niantic-pokemon-go-spin-out

21 Ben Grubb, "Just Add a Smartphone: Google Cardboard Headset Revolutionises DIY Virtual Reality," *Sydney Morning Herald*, June 27, 2014, https://www.smh.com.au/technology/just-add-a-smartphone-google-cardboard-headset-revolutionises-diy-virtual-reality-20140627-zsnly.html

22 Mark Pesce, "Virtual Reality Is Actually Made out of Smartphones," The Register, October 13, 2016, https://www.theregister.co.uk/2016/10/13/virtual_reality_is_made_of_smartphones/

Chapter 2: Surveillance Status

1 Mark Pesce and Dr. Genevieve Bell, "1968: When the World Began," PodcastOne, Australia 2018, https://nextbillionseconds.com/1968-when-the-world-began/

2 Jessi Hempel, "Project HoloLens: Our Exclusive Hands-On with Microsoft's Holographic Goggles," WIRED, January 21, 2015, https://www.wired.com/2015/01/microsoft-hands-on/

3 Mark Pesce, "The Xbox: 1,000,000,000,000 Operations per Second," WIRED, May 1, 2001, https://www.wired.com/2001/05/xbox/

4 Tom Kim, "In-Depth: Eye to Eye – The History of EyeToy," Gamasutra, November 6, 2008, https://www.gamasutra.com/view/news/111925/InDepth_Eye_To_Eye__The_History_Of_EyeToy.php

5 A tutorial on SLAM – suitable for non-technical readers – can be found here: https://www.kudan.io/post/an-introduction-to-simultaneous-localisation-and-mapping

6 Adam Tuliper, "Introduction to HoloLens, Part 2: Spatial Mapping," *Microsoft Developer Network*, January 2017, https://docs.microsoft.com/en-us/archive/msdn-magazine/2017/january/hololens-introduction-to-the-hololens-part-2-spatial-mapping

7 Raymond Wong, "HoloLens' Worst Enemy Is Still Itself," Mashable, May 9, 2018, https://mashable.com/2018/05/08/microsoft-hololens-field-of-view-big-weakness/

8 Microsoft Developer Network, "Mapping Physical Spaces with HoloLens," September 16, 2019, https://docs.microsoft.com/en-us/hololens/hololens-spaces

9 Sean Hollister and Rebecca Fleenor, "How Pokemon Go Affects your Phone's Battery Life and Data," CNET, July 13, 2016, https://www.cnet.com/how-to/pokemon-go-battery-test-data-usage/

10 Dyani Sabin, "The Secret History of 'Pokemon Go' as Told by Creator John Hanke," Inverse, February 28, 2017, https://www.inverse.com/article/28485-pokemon-go-secret-history-google-maps-ingress-john-hanke-updates

11 Mark Pesce, "Minecraft's My Nirvana. I Found It Hard, It's Hard to Find. Oh Well, Whatever... Never Mined...," *The Register*, May 23, 2019, https://www.theregister.co.uk/2019/05/23/column_may/

12 Samuel Gibbs, "Google Glass Advice: How to Avoid Being a Glasshole," *The Guardian*, February 19, 2014,

https://www.theguardian.com/technology/2014/
feb/19/google-glass-advice-smartglasses-glasshole

13 Steven Winkelman, "Apple AR glasses: News and
Rumours about 'Project Mirrorshades', Yahoo!
Finance, August 31, 2018, https://finance.yahoo.
com/news/apple-project-mirrorshades-news-
rumors-144108933.html

14 TechKnock, "Facebook F8 2017 Keynote Day 1,"
https://www.youtube.com/watch?v=n0QdQ3rz
WNs

15 Mark Pesce and Tony Parisi, "The Next Billion
Seconds: Virtual Real," PodcastOne, Australia,
May 30, 2018, https://nextbillionseconds.com/
2018/05/30/episode-2-06-virtually-real-with-tony-
parisi/

16 James Vincent, "Apple Reportedly Plans 2022
Release for First AR Headset, Followed by AR
Glasses in 2023," *The Verge*, November 11, 2019,
https://www.theverge.com/2019/11/11/20959066/
apple-augmented-reality-ar-headset-glasses-ru-
mors-reported-release-date

17 J. C. Torres, "Oppo AR Glasses Hands-On,"
Slashgear, December 19, 2019, https://www.
slashgear.com/oppo-ar-glasses-hands-on-oppos-
future-vision-10602757/

Chapter 3: The Last Days of Reality

1 James Surowiecki, "Where Nokia Went
Wrong," *The New Yorker*, September 3, 2013,
https://www.newyorker.com/business/currency/
where-nokia-went-wrong

2 Arne Holst, "Number of Smartphone Users Worldwide from 2016 to 2021," Statista, November 11, 2019, https://www.statista.com/statistics/330695/number-of-smartphone-users-worldwide/

3 "To do with the price of fish," *The Economist*, May 10, 2007, https://www.economist.com/finance-and-economics/2007/05/10/to-do-with-the-price-of-fish

4 Waldrop, *The Dream Machine*, pp. 333–410.

5 Tim Berners-Lee, "Information Management: A Proposal," CERN, March 1989, https://cds.cern.ch/record/1405411/files/ARCH-WWW-4-010.pdf

6 Mark Pesce, *The Playful World: How Technology is Transforming Our Imagination* (New York: Ballantine Books, 2000), pp. 194–5.

7 "The World Wide Web Hall of Fame," 1994, https://botw.org/1994/awards/fame.html

8 Shoshanna Zuboff, *The Age of Surveillance Capitalism* (New York: Public Affairs, 2019), pp. 63–81.

9 Claire Groden, "Here's How Many Americans Sleep with their Smartphones," Forbes, June 30, 2015, https://fortune.com/2015/06/29/sleep-banks-smartphones/

10 Nicholas Carlson, "Well, These New Zuckerberg IMs Won't Help Facebook's Privacy Problems," *Business Insider*, May 14, 2010, https://www.businessinsider.com/well-these-new-zuckerberg-ims-wont-help-facebooks-privacy-problems-2010-5?IR=T

11 Nicholas Christakis and James H. Fowler, "Social Contagion Theory: Examining Dynamic Social Networks and Human Behaviour," *Statistics in*

Medicine, June 18, 2012, https://doi.org/10.1002/sim.5408

12 Zuboff, *The Age of Surveillance Capitalism*, p. 92.

13 Mark Pesce, "The Last Days of Reality," Meanjin, Summer 2017, https://meanjin.com.au/essays/the-last-days-of-reality/

14 Robinson Meyer, "Everything We Know About Facebook's Secret Mood Manipulation Experiment," *The Atlantic*, June 28, 2014, https://www.theatlantic.com/technology/archive/2014/06/everything-we-know-about-facebooks-secret-mood-manipulation-experiment/373648/

15 Darren Davidson, "Facebook Exploits 'Insecure' Teens to Sell Ads," *The Australian*, May 1, 2017.

16 Carole Cadwalladr, "Fresh Cambridge Analytica Leak 'Shows Global Manipulation Is out of Control'," *The Guardian*, January 4, 2020, https://www.theguardian.com/uk-news/2020/jan/04/cambridge-analytica-data-leak-global-election-manipulation?CMP=share_btn_tw&__twitter_impression=true

17 Tiffany Shlain, *24/6: The Power of Unplugging One Day a Week* (New York: Gallery Books, 2019), pp. 38–47.

18 David Goldman, "Google Unveils 'Project Glass' Virtual-Reality Glasses," CNN Money, April 4, 2012, https://money.cnn.com/2012/04/04/technology/google-project-glass/index.htm?iid=EL

19 Charles Arthur, "Google's Sergey Brin: Smartphones Are 'Emasculating'," *The Guardian*, March 1, 2013, https://www.theguardian.com/technology/2013/feb/28/google-sergey-brin-smartphones-emasculating

20 Sherry Turkle, *Alone Together: Why We Expect More from Technology and Less from Each Other* (New York: Basic Books, 2011).

21 Peter Rubin, "Eye Tracking is Coming to VR Sooner Than You Think. What Now?," WIRED, March 23, 2018, https://www.wired.com/story/eye-tracking-vr/

22 Ben Lang, "Eye-tracking is a Game-Changer for VR That Goes Far Beyond Foveated Rendering," Road to VR, May 9, 2018, https://www.roadtovr.com/why-eye-tracking-is-a-game-changer-for-vr-headsets-virtual-reality/

23 Blake J. Harris, *The History of the Future: Oculus, Facebook and the Revolution that Swept Virtual Reality* (New York: William Morrow, 2018), pp. 409–27.

24 Michael Kan, "Facebook: Your Oculus VR Data Can Now Be Used for Ad Targeting," *PC Magazine*, December 11, 2019, https://www.pcmag.com/news/facebook-your-oculus-vr-data-can-now-be-used-for-ad-targeting

25 Mark Pesce, "Sense and Sensors," *IEEE Spectrum*, February 2020.

Chapter 4: The Web Wide World

1 Chip Morningstar and Randy Farmer, "The Lessons of Lucasfilm's Habitat," in M. Benedikt, ed., *Cyberspace: First Steps* (Cambridge, MA: MIT Press, 1990), pp. 273–302.

2 Daisy Dumas, "Australian Rock Art May Be Among Oldest in the World, According to New

Research," *Sydney Morning Herald*, February 20, 2016, https://www.smh.com.au/national/australian-rock-may-be-among-the-oldest-in-the-world-according-to-new-research-20160219-gmyaw1.html

3 David Rapp, "Inventing Yahoo," American Heritage, April 12, 2006, https://web.archive.org/web/20100716081021/http://www.americanheritage.com/events/articles/web/20060412-yahoo-internet-search-engine-jerry-yang-david-filo-america-online-google-ipo-email.shtml

4 Claire Broadley, "AltaVista – The Tragic Tale of the Search Engine Pioneer," Digital.com, November 6, 2019, https://digital.com/about/altavista/

5 Sergey Brin and Larry Page, "The Anatomy of a Large-Scale Hypertextual Web Search Engine," *Computer Networks and ISDN Systems*, 30, 1–7, April 1998, 107–17.

6 Matthew Gault, "Farmers are Buying 40-Year-Old Tractors Because They're Actually Repairable," VICE, January 20, 2020, https://www.vice.com/en_au/article/bvgx9w/farmers-are-buying-40-year-old-tractors-because-theyre-actually-repairable

7 Michel Foucault, *Discipline and Punish: The Birth of the Prison* (New York: Pantheon Books, 1977).

8 Mark Pesce, "Sure, HoloLens Is Cute, but Ford Was Making VR Work before It Was Cool," *The Register*, September 18, 2017, https://www.theregister.co.uk/2017/09/18/ford_virtual_reality/

9 Tony Parisi, "Building the Mirrorworld," afterword to *Creating Augmented and Virtual Realities* (Sebastopol, CA: O'Reilly Press, 2019).

10 Mark Pesce, "The Rise of the Replicators," Medium.com, October 19, 2017, https://medium.com/@mpesce/rise-of-the-replicators-4011fcc015c7
11 Ludwig Wittgenstein, *Tractatus Logico-Philosophicus* (London: Routledge, 1922).
12 Pesce, *The Playful World*, pp. 73–90.
13 Rapp, "Inventing Yahoo."
14 Kalyeena Makortoff, "Google Owner Alphabet Becomes Trillion-Dollar Company," *The Guardian*, January 17, 2020, https://www.theguardian.com/technology/2020/jan/17/google-owner-alphabet-becomes-trillion-dollar-company
15 Eli Pariser, *The Filter Bubble: What the Internet is Hiding From You* (New York: Penguin, 2011).
16 Although commonly attributed to Marshall McLuhan, this quote seems to have originated with Father John Culkin.

Chapter 5: Setting the World to Writes

1 Transcription of the F8 2017 keynote, video of which can be found at https://www.youtube.com/watch?v=n0QdQ3rzWNs
2 Mike Issac, "Mark Zuckerberg Sees Augmented Reality Ecosystem in Facebook," *The New York Times*, April 18, 2017, https://www.nytimes.com/2017/04/18/technology/mark-zuckerberg-sees-augmented-reality-ecosystem-in-facebook.html
3 danah boyd, *It's Complicated: The Social Lives of Networked Teens* (New Haven, CT: Yale University Press, 2014).

4 Zachary Jason, "Game of Fear," *Boston Magazine*, April 28, 2015, https://www.bostonmagazine.com/news/2015/04/28/gamergate/3/#.VUCLfGxC2MA.twitter

5 Alex Schiffer, "Should Augmented Reality Games Like 'Pokémon Go' Place Limits on the Real World Locations They Include?," *Los Angeles Times*, July 20, 2016, https://www.latimes.com/business/la-fi-tn-pokemon-opt-out-20160715-snap-story.html

6 Mark Pesce, "Hyperpolitics (American Style)," Edge.org, February 2, 2008, https://www.edge.org/conversation/mark_pesce-hyperpolitics-american-style

7 Matt Miesnieks, "The AR Cloud Will Be Bigger Than Search," Forbes, January 4, 2018, https://www.forbes.com/sites/charliefink/2018/01/04/the-arcloud-will-be-bigger-than-search/#2d757d1a4e8f

8 Michelle Starr, "Pokemon Go Perfect Storm Turns Tiny Park into Suburban Nightmare," CNET, July 24, 2016, https://www.cnet.com/news/pokemon-go-perfect-storm-turns-tiny-park-into-suburban-nightmare/

9 Michel Bauwens and Vasilis Narios, *Value in the Commons Economy: Developments in Open and Contributory Value Accounting* (Chiang Mai: Heinrich-Böll Foundation, 2017), pp. 11–15.

10 Walter Chen, "How Pokemon Go is Driving Insane Amounts of Sales at Small, Local Businesses," *Inc.*, July 11, 2016, https://www.inc.com/walter-chen/pok-mon-go-is-driving-insane-amounts-of-sales-at-small-local-businesses-here-s-h.html

11 A. J. Dellinger, "'Pokémon Go' Settlement Promises Action on Nuisance Pokéstops," Engadget, February

25, 2019, https://www.engadget.com/2019/02/15/
niantic-pokemon-go-trespassing-lawsuit-settlement/

12 Eriq Gardner, "'Pokemon Go' Creator Agrees to
Tighter Leash on Virtual Creatures to End Class
Action," *The Hollywood Reporter*, February 15,
2019, https://www.hollywoodreporter.com/thr-esq/
pokemon-go-creator-agrees-tighter-leash-virtual-
creatures-end-class-action-1187097

13 Matthew Field, "Drone Standards Aim to Regulate
the 'Wild West' of Airspace," *The Telegraph*,
November 21, 2018, https://www.telegraph.co.uk/
technology/2018/11/21/first-ever-global-drone-
standards-aim-regulate-wild-west-airspace/

14 Jake Evans, "Drone's 'Flyer's License' to be
Launched in Time for Google's World-First Delivery
Service in Canberra," ABC News, March 27,
2019, https://www.abc.net.au/news/2019-03-27/
drone-licences-to-be-issued-ahead-of-canberra-
delivery-service/10943284?section=business

15 P. Mockapetris, "Domain Names – Implementation
and Specification," IETF Network Working Group
Request for Comment document 1035, November
1987, https://www.ietf.org/rfc/rfc1035.txt

16 In 2016, the author proposed one potential
solution to handle the technology of permissions
for locative metadata, the Mixed Reality Service
(MRS), described at https://mixedrealityservice.org

Index

Illustrations are indicated by page numbers in italics.

Index

Index

Index

Index

Index

Index